COMING HOME

My Amazin' Life with the New York Mets

Cleon Jones

with Gary Kaschak

TRIUMPH
BOOKS

Library of Congress Cataloging-in-Publication Data

Names: Jones, Cleon, 1942– author. | Kaschak, Gary, author.
Title: Coming home: my amazin' life with the New York Mets / Cleon Jones, with Gary Kaschak; [foreword by Ron Swoboda].
Other titles: My amazing life with the New York Mets
Description: Chicago, IL: Triumph Books, [2022] | Summary: "This book is the autobiography of former New York Mets star Cleon Jones"—Provided by publisher.
Identifiers: LCCN 2022005650 | ISBN 9781637270073 (Hardcover)
Subjects: LCSH: Jones, Cleon, 1942– | Baseball players—United States—Biography. | New York Mets (Baseball team)—History. | World Series (Baseball) (1969) | Baseball—Alabama—History. | Africatown (Ala.)—History. | Clotilda (Ship)—History. | BISAC: BIOGRAPHY & AUTOBIOGRAPHY / Sports | HISTORY / United States / State & Local / South (AL, AR, FL, GA, KY, LA, MS, NC, SC, TN, VA, WV)
Classification: LCC GV865.J64 A34 2022 | DDC 796.357092 [B]—dc23/eng/20220223
LC record available at https://lccn.loc.gov/2022005650

This book is available in quantity at special discounts for your group or organization. For further information, contact:

Triumph Books LLC
814 North Franklin Street
Chicago, IL 60610
(312) 337-0747
www.triumphbooks.com

Printed in the United States of America
ISBN: 978-1-63727-007-3
Design and editorial production by Alex Lubertozzi
Photos courtesy of AP Images unless otherwise indicated

Contents

Foreword

AS A WHITE KID growing up in Baltimore County, a thoroughly segregated community, circa 1960s, arriving in St. Petersburg, Florida, in 1964 for my first taste of professional baseball was a bit of a culture shock. I hadn't played with or against any Black players in my amateur career to date and didn't know a soul from the Deep South. I knew Cleon was from Mobile, Alabama, where a ton of great major leaguers were born and raised, guys like Hank Aaron, Willie McCovey, Billy Williams, and former Mets like Tommie Agee and Amos Otis. If you expand that list to the state of Alabama, the numbers will blow your mind.

What rocked me was watching Cleon at home plate. While I was hoping I had something to offer the professional game, Cleon looked like somebody who had figured it out. At the time, it never occurred to me to approach him about hitting because, honestly, coming from the eastern part of the country, with Cleon's Deep South drawl, the words came fast and furious at first—I had no clue what he was talking about.

Fortunately, we got to spend a fair amount of time together off the field, and my ear eventually became tuned to Cleon's patois, and I was a better person for it. It turns out we had a lot in common. Coming from Baltimore County, I was hip to the seafood economy around the Chesapeake Bay with its bounty of blue crabs, fish, and oysters. Coming from Mobile, Cleon knew all about blue crabs—except they boiled them there in a zesty broth, and we Marylanders cooked the crabs with live steam in a pot with a heavy and hot, spicy coating. Bottom line was when my mom and dad came up to New York with a mess of Maryland steamed crabs, Cleon knew how to crack them and eat them by the dozen. Mix in a couple of cold beers, and Cleon might launch into a tale about a friend from home who would catch fish if you just turned on the faucet. And those were good times.

They got better in 1969 when the Mets matured quietly into a contender, and Cleon, with a few major league seasons under his belt, vaulted into the National League batting race with the likes of Pete Rose and Roberto Clemente. It was always interesting to me that the only hitting aid we had back then were some loops of 16mm film that you could project on the wall in this little back room off of our clubhouse. The only person I ever saw in there, feeding the loops through the projector aimed at the wall in little images that looked like 1950s television, was Cleon Jones. I couldn't spend five minutes in that constricted place. Cleon told me recently that he watched more than his own at-bats. "I watched other guys when they were going good and what they were doing at the plate, and when they were going bad figuring out the things that were keeping them from hitting the ball good." The .340 average that Cleon posted put him just behind Clemente at .345 and Rose, leading the way at .348. As they might say in Alabama, that was tall cotton.

There's no doubt in my mind that Cleon helped his Mobile homeboy Tommie Agee rebound offensively from an awful 1968. As a student of hitting, you glean things from everywhere. I credit Tommy Davis, who was a Met in 1967, with helping me to my best batting average of .280 just by being in the batting order ahead of me and getting me better pitches to hit. But Cleon was in the graduate level of hitting. "Tommy Davis and I talked a lot," Cleon said. "His point was that the body was just support for the hitting mechanism, the hands were the weapons." In those hands Cleon carried a large piece of wood up to home plate and what he could do with 37 or 38 ounces of northern ash spoke loudly.

I, on the other hand, floundered offensively through the first half of 1969. And with Gil Hodges, you hit or you sit. Pretty simple. Funny thing was, Cleon was having some trouble with his ankle, and we were having some trouble with the Astros. Houston beat the crap out of us in 1969. They won 10 of 12 games we played, and on Wednesday, July 30, in Shea Stadium it only got worse. After Houston strapped a 16–3 bruising on us in Game 1, we were down 10–0 in Game 2 after Johnny Edwards doubled in Doug Rader from first base. I was on the pines, where I belonged, but that would change.

Much was written about what happened next. The writers covering the team seemed to focus on what they thought was Cleon's lack of hustle after Edwards' line drive down the left-field line. Gil Hodges took the slowest walk you've ever seen by a manager who had some distance to cover. Gil walked by the pitcher, Nolan Ryan, a Texan taking his turn at getting shellacked by Houston. Past our shortstop, Bud Harrelson, who breathed a big sigh of relief. And on to left field, where Gil had a prolonged discussion with Cleon and finally lifted him from the game and put me into left field. Cleon all these years later tells me the conversation was never accusatory, never berating. Cleon told me, "He asked me if I was hurt, and I told him to look at the water that back then tended to collect in the outfield at Shea and how muddy it was." And when Gil suggested maybe Cleon should leave the game, Cleon agreed. Today, as he did back then, Cleon felt like "he had a motive to shake the team up." We've talked about this before, and I think Gil looked around the dugout and didn't see anybody too upset about us having our butts handed to us by the Astros and made one of the most impressive scenes of the season purely for effect. I'm here to tell you, it worked.

The 1969 New York Mets went on a roll, winning close to three out of every four games, running down the Chicago Cubs, who were leading the National League East all year, and we never looked back. I went on a useful offensive run that lasted through August and September and into the World Series. Cleon was back into the lineup after his ankle calmed down, and he continued the kind of hitting that led us to a World Series win.

We've stayed friends for more than a half-century now. And he has only grown from the man and the player that he was with the Mets—back home in Africatown, Alabama, which was absorbed into Mobile, and historically is where the last cargo of Africans for delivery into slavery occurred in 1860. Cleon's work with the Africatown Development Corporation, painting homes and replacing roofs for folks who would otherwise do without, only shows the heart and soul of a man who will never forget where he came from and will never quit trying to make it a better place.

—Ron Swoboda

Introduction

WHEN I WAS 12 years old in 1968, we lived in the Binghamton, New York, area, raised as Yankees fans right at the end of their pennant-winning years. There were no issues whatsoever rooting for the Yankees and the Mets together, no beating on the chest to say one team was better than the other because neither one was.

The first game I ever attended was at Shea Stadium that year, a 1–0 loss to the Astros on a Jimmy Wynn home run in the sixth. I was entirely interested in the game despite the lack of offense. For the longest time I remembered the starting lineups, memorized each player's number as well as the announced attendance. When I looked it up, I tried recalling what it was, and I was close, missing it by just a few hundred people.

A year later, we all became Mets fans. We started following the standings and watching the games on WOR, watching *Kiner's Korner*, completely entranced by what was happening. I followed the box scores of all the games and memorized the statistics of players from the Sunday paper, and one of them was Cleon Jones.

I rooted for Cleon as much as I did the Mets. He was leading the league in batting for most of the season, and then the injuries came. But I hadn't given up on him. In my young mind I thought he could hit .400 and win the batting crown easily. It didn't matter to me that Pete Rose or Roberto Clemente or any of those other guys were challenging him. It didn't matter at all. And as that season progressed and ended with the same kind of magic we'd experienced all season, we were elated beyond words. And I wasn't upset that Cleon hadn't won the batting crown—there'd be other years.

Never in my imagination did I ever think I'd meet Cleon Jones or, for that matter, collaborate on his book. But a series of events only a few years ago changed all that, and as I think about it now, I'm still in wonder.

My wife and I were watching the news a few years ago when the announcer started talking about a discovery in Mobile Bay of the *Clotilda*—a vessel from Civil War times involved in the illegal transport of enslaved people out of Africa. A few seconds later, they mentioned that "Ex–New York Met Cleon Jones was involved in its discovery."

We watched Cleon climb out of that boat to see for himself what had been found. I was as interested now as I was in the 1969 Mets for a number of reasons.

I'd written a historical novel called *Lifestone* several years earlier that featured the *Clotilda* in early chapters. It was quite an unusual coincidence that one of my heroes was interested in a topic I'd written about. I remember saying to my wife, Maureen, "I wish there was some way I could talk to Cleon about this," but I never tried reaching him.

About a year ago the executive director for the New York State Baseball Hall of Fame, Rene LeRoux, named me editor of its new newsletter. My first interview was with Dodgers great Carl Erskine, and then it was Cleon Jones. I was excited to get the chance to talk with him about baseball, but our first order of business would be the *Clotilda*. I told Cleon my story, and we hit it off right away.

I followed up a few weeks later and asked him if he'd considered writing a book. From what he'd had to say, there was a lot inside of him. He seemed fine with the concept, so I contacted Triumph Books with the idea, told them some things about Cleon they didn't know, and before long, we had a deal.

Several months and interviews later, Cleon's wife, Angela, picked up the phone following one of our interviews and said she had something to tell me.

"I want you to know something," she said. "The day you called and asked Cleon if he was interested in writing a book with you, we were having breakfast together, talking about things. I told him right there at breakfast that he had a story to tell and should tell it. It wasn't five minutes later when you called. This was a divine intervention."

Whether it be incredible luck, serendipity, or a divine intervention, it has been my honor and privilege to work with this man and to grow close with both of them. He does have a story to tell, and we hope you enjoy reading it as much as I enjoyed learning about it.

And I would be remiss if I did not thank my friends Sean Holtz of the Baseball Almanac for researching hard-to-find facts and Rene LeRoux for believing in me and introducing me to Cleon Jones. And especially to fellow author Alan Maimon for offering a word of advice and providing support and confidence through the many valleys traveled prior to this project.

—Gary Kaschak
December 27, 2021

Chapter 1

THE LAST OUT

THE NIGHT BEFORE the fifth game of the 1969 World Series was when I first started thinking about what was about to happen. We'd won three straight games against the highly favored Baltimore Orioles and had a chance to win it—to win it all—before our home fans at Shea Stadium. We all knew that if we lost we'd be going back to Baltimore for at least Game 6, and none of us wanted that to happen. We wanted to win at home. There was a lot going through my mind that night.

As a player in your down time, you leave the field physically, but you don't leave the field mentally. So much goes through your mind—what's going to happen tomorrow, and what situation are you going to be in to make a difference? So it was rare that I found myself contemplating like I did that night. I was always focused on the game and never let any of the distractions that come with the territory—especially playing in the World Series—throw me off my game. And being that we were on the eve of playing what turned out to be the most important game of our lives, focusing on the game at hand was in the forefront. But I couldn't help but let my mind wander some. I'm sure none of us could.

Thinking about losing Game 5 never crossed my mind. Winning only crossed my mind. As I started thinking about Game 5, I thought about all my teammates and how each had played a part in winning games that season, some of them improbable and some even hard to believe.

I thought about what Gil Hodges had told us in spring training, that we were "better than we thought we were," and how we all kind of looked at each other and wondered what he was talking about. I thought of the many times during the season Gil had pushed all the right buttons, and never seemed surprised when something worked out.

Certain games crossed my mind. The Black Cat game. Seaver's near-perfect game. The doubleheader against Pittsburgh when Jerry Koosman and Don Cardwell each won 1–0, with each driving in the game's only run. I thought further back to our 11-game winning streak; the day we went over .500; and the magical, surreal day we went into first place for good, getting goosebumps when seeing the National League East standings posted on the scoreboard at Shea.

I thought about the great catches made just a few days earlier by Tommie Agee and Ron Swoboda, how Swoboda had practiced for that one play all season long and never made even one catch. I thought about the black shoe polish game...and I thought about our fans and that we were finally going to give them justice. But through it all, I never thought I'd make the last catch of the Series. It never crossed my mind at all. I never imagined myself driving in the winning run or being the star of the game. My focus was on getting good at-bats, staying within myself, contributing what I could to my team, and winning the game.

When Davey Johnson connected on Jerry Koosman's final pitch of the game and Series, and that ball sailed toward me in left field, Koosman thought it was a home run, and so did Davey Johnson. But I knew from the moment the ball left his bat that it was staying in the park. I took one step back and realized the ball was in front of me and wasn't even going to make it to the warning track. I made a couple steps in then got under the ball and said, "Come on down, baby...come on down, baby...now it's over."

It's hard to explain the many thoughts a mind can have at such moments, and I've never shared some of mine until now. All I know is when that fly ball reached its peak, it seemed suspended in mid-air for just a moment. As it made its way down into my glove, I wasn't thinking at all about dropping to my knee. What I thought about was all the National League fans, especially all the old Brooklyn Dodgers fans and the New York Giant fans who'd lost an entire franchise just a few years earlier, and how hard that must have been. Most everybody who became Mets fans were either Brooklyn Dodgers or New York Giant fans, and we were constantly reminded of that by people who came from the Bronx or other places to see us play at Shea. These were mostly diehard National League fans, and hardly any switched allegiance to the Yankees.

Certainly there was no Jackie Robinson, Pee Wee Reese, Junior Gilliam, Duke Snider, Willie Mays, or Monte Irving to root for, but those players and others had to be on their minds. But in the ever-changing world of baseball, they had new players like Tom Seaver, Jerry Koosman, Jerry Grote, Bud Harrelson, Ron Swoboda, and even a Cleon Jones to root for. Maybe—just maybe—we took away some of the hurt losing an entire team can do to a city.

When the ball came down, I thought about our Mets fans who'd been with us since 1962, how faithful and trusting they'd been to us. To have the patience and the fortitude to stick with losers, so to speak, was on my mind. We were finally going to give the fans justice. Not only that, we were going to be a winner for all New Yorkers. Be a winner for the underdogs. Be a winner for the country, and even the world. God knows what made me get into the position I was in and to kneel as that ball entered my glove. It was a sigh of relief and it was a moment of gratitude. There's a lot of things you can't explain in life, and that's one of them. I didn't go to the outfield in the last inning thinking to make the last out or falling to my knee. But I'm thankful that I did.

I've always said that if you spend sufficient time on your knees, you'll have no trouble standing on your feet. I had always been taught that kneeling signifies and suggests prayer, and being sensitive and symbolic to prayer and the supreme being. As that Shea Stadium crowd understood what was about to happen when that ball began its descent, I had a fixation on just that. Catching the ball, giving thanks and falling to my knee.

But beyond all the baseball and beyond all the cheering and the noise and the elation and celebrating that followed, it was my community and its people—past and present—that shared all that space of gratitude I was feeling. All these years later I have thought of that catch on occasion, and when I do, I take a moment to reflect and imagine if only time could've stood still for just that moment—a moment with no other players on the field, no fans in the stands, no jets overhead, no noise whatsoever. Just me.

I would've stayed on my knee for a while, thinking about all of that, grateful and humbled to have reached such a point in life. Grateful to my community for being my guiding force, to show me the way, for encouraging me and coaching me, for recognizing my God-given talents and providing what was needed to succeed.

I would have paid homage to my ancestors, those who came from Africa just before the Civil War, enslaved people stolen from their homes by greedy, Godless people—heartless people guided only by profit and gain with no regard for humanity and the basic rights of all people.

I would have thanked all 110 of them who settled here in Africatown for having the fortitude and the desire and whatever faith they'd known before to build again, to start over, and to leave a legacy that lives on, and I would have thanked Jackie Robinson for opening doors for people of color, for enduring all the hardships he faced as he paved the way for us.

It's hard to believe that more than 50 years have gone by since I caught that ball. I never imagined that the image of me going down to a partial knee-drop would be an image that has stayed in the minds and hearts of Mets fans all these years later. I never thought at the time how significant that final image would be in ways I couldn't even imagine, that years later I would build my Last Out Foundation nonprofit to help our local residents in dire need—our brothers and sisters—and to be representing New York, the Mets, and my community in so doing.

Perhaps Providence had lent a helping hand. Davey Johnson said it was the hardest ball he'd ever hit, and later said there must have been some divine intervention on that play. Jerry Koosman said he thought it was a sure home run.

There's so much we cannot explain, how one event links to another and then another, and believing in the process formed by the Almighty to make things happen in his time.

Who knew that the "Miracle Mets" season of 1969 would live on in ways none of us imagined back then, and in many ways how that one unforgettable season was a coming home for so many.

Chapter 2

THE APPLES OF LIFE

I HAVE ALWAYS been the kind of person who was happiest to be home. To me, home meant comfort, security, relaxation, and always was the place I wanted to be most. I never thought much about how often I wanted to come home and stay home until we started reminiscing about it. Then when I first saw the words "Coming Home" written across the cover page of the manuscript for this book, I found it to be gratifying and appropriate.

There's a saying everybody knows—"Home is where the heart is"—and that couldn't be more true in describing what's in my heart and has always been in my heart for my community of Africatown (also called Plateau) in Mobile, Alabama. When I think back with all that's happened in my life and understanding what transpired to make me what I became, I hold a deep gratitude to so many members of our community who took the time to be a guiding force in my life.

Some of my heroes are bigger than life—characters like Jackie Robinson, Larry Doby, Joe Louis, Jessie Owens, Martin Luther King Jr., and W.E.B. Du Bois. I think about all of these people who were forerunners and had a mandate. They were somehow able to reach the goal they were after with nothing but a desire and a support system. Sometimes you have to reach down in yourself and pull out the strength that you know God gave you in order to succeed. How else could Jackie Robinson do what he did? How else could Jesse Owens go to Germany, being hated the way he was hated, and perform at such a high level—then come back home, have a dinner in his honor, and have to go through the back door to get to his own banquet? It is these men and many others—both men and women—who sometimes took drastic measures and put their lives on the line who drive me to make things better. What they did was vitally important and has stayed inside me in everything I do.

But other heroes, for me, are names most people don't know. They're names that are part of the fabric a community is made up of. Difference makers who have recognized a need and are willing to do what it takes, to go that extra mile in cultivating and inspiring and affecting a young mind. Names like Mrs. Valena McCants and Mama Myrt.

Mrs. McCants was a Godsend. She was a teacher that you had once in a lifetime—if you were so lucky. She made a difference in our lives by showing us the way. Some people might have had some misgivings about the importance of a quality education, but she was drawn to them and sought them out and showed us a different way. I was one of those people.

I had no real aspirations of going to college. All I ever heard in my upbringing from my grandmother and my great-grandmother was that they only went to the fourth or fifth grade, and the only book in my house was the Bible. When that's all you've known all your life, you start thinking the same for yourself, and need someone to recognize that way of thinking and to intercede. The driving force in my life certainly wasn't education, it was athletics, and Mrs. McCants knew that.

But I knew that if I wanted to partake in any and all of the athletics, I had to partake in education. Athletics was my driving force, and Mrs. McCants encouraged me to play, but she implored me to think about more than sports, to balance out athletics with education. She stressed that, even with athletic talent good enough for professional sports, the time in sports would be fleeting, whereas an education would be forever. She wanted us to learn to give back to our own families, to remember our roots, and to be thankful for what we have and give back to society in ways that went far beyond money.

She was a history teacher, but she was a counselor to many of us. Thank God she was someone who took her job seriously and took us seriously. She made it a point to know all your family members and all those at the school, and all of those who came before them. She had an influence over us because she knew who we were and where we came from, and she could always call everyone's name and compare us to others from our family. That's the way she inspired us.

She ruled with an iron hand. Early on she was the kind of teacher who would tug on your ear even if you were 6'9" and weighed 300 pounds. If you were in the school hallway when you weren't supposed to be, she'd either pull on your ear or take her heel and step on your foot. I used to tell her all the time, "You can step on my foot all you want. You can wear out the top because the bottom is already worn out." She thought that was funny.

She got to you before you got in trouble. There was a store across the street we used to slip off campus to, and sometimes other students would see me there and tell her. She'd find me and say, "You know you're not supposed to go off campus," and she would take my ear lobe and straighten me out, not afraid my caregiver would find out because she had the blessings of all the parents and all the grandparents to do that to all of us. It didn't matter how big you were or how bad you thought you were, she would get in your chest and straighten you out. That's the kind of neighborhood I grew up in back then—and when you got home you got another switch.

If Mrs. McCants told me to go tell my grandmother I'd done something wrong, I wouldn't hide it because that would have made matters worse. And because my grandmother worked as a cook at the school, she knew if I got a paddling at school she'd be the first to know and be ready for me when I got home to get another one. At that time principals and vice-principals could paddle you. If the principal or vice-principal or any teacher said I'd done something wrong, my grandmother didn't question it— she knew I did it, and I wouldn't lie to her. I told her I did it and I was sorry—sorry because I was worried about getting a whupping.

Today we still have a wonderful relationship with her—she's 97 years of age, lives just a few miles from us, and we speak to her almost daily or stop by to see her and how she's doing.

Mama Myrt, my grandmother, read from the Bible to us, and we went to church every Sunday like everybody else in the area did. We learned at home and in church that the Bible was the equalizer. By that I mean, whenever somebody told you something about the Bible you took that to heart because it was coming from God Almighty. It was part of our daily life and what we believed in. And the preachers lived in the neighborhood and preached every day of the week—not just on Sunday.

Since Sunday was the one day of the week we went to church, the one day we were "religious," I told most of my friends that if they died any day but Sunday, they're surely going to hell because the other six days they lived life like a wrecking ball. If Sunday was your day to die, you might have a chance to go to heaven. I truly believed that.

There are so many examples like these that rubbed off on me and helped me to better understand what a real community can be. What I think about all the time is: you're a product of your community. Everybody thinks it's all about you, but often times it's about everything but you. In my case, it's about my community because I've always looked at my community as a team. That might sound far-fetched to some, but in my community everybody looked out for one another. Before we ever heard the phrase "my brother's keeper," we were our brothers' keepers. Certainly you would not be talking about Cleon Jones as a major league baseball player had I not been born and raised in this small, tight-knit community of caring people.

The thing is, people say Cleon Jones made Africatown known. No, Africatown made Cleon Jones. That's in my heart because people need to know it's not about you, it's about everything else—what you're surrounded by and what you take in. It's like going to school every day and getting all you can out of it to make it work for you. A safe haven to further your development and a space and an avenue to help develop your skill and the mind power to be able to develop in a way that you can even become a major league player.

As a person and a player you owe all that to your community. That's what happened to me as it relates to sports. The tutelage was so enormous because it wasn't one or two people, it was a community. Home was always the driving force for me. To me, home meant family, and my whole community was my family. I never had thoughts of whether I would fail because I was representing a community that had been so supportive of me as an athlete—a son of this neighborhood. My inspiration came from that because it was sort of instilled in me. I always got energized from what I got from my neighbors and friends.

Long before any of these people came into my life, I was just a child living in the Deep South with an older brother, my parents, and grandmother. I found out soon enough that there was something unique about my given name. It didn't take long for me to discover that I was the only boy around with the name of Cleon.

But I paid no mind to it. It was a big world out there, and there were other Cleons in it. All I knew then was that it was different.

One of my kids looked it up one day and said it was of Greek origin and means "glory" and "famous," or "renowned." Turns out Cleon was a Greek general from an aristocratic family who opposed the Spartans. As I read more about him, I was drawn to the fact that he was concerned and had empathy for the lower class, and I found that very fitting because this Cleon shares those very same ideals. I used to make a statement, "How could a boy from Africatown, Alabama, named Cleon Jones make it to the major leagues, let alone win a World Series and play in an All-Star Game?"

I don't know if my mother got my name out of a magazine or what, because I never got the chance to talk with her. She moved to Philadelphia when I was just two years old to make a new start and died there years later after living with her great aunt. There was a lot of that kind of thing going on in the South. People were running for their lives and seeking employment elsewhere, migrating to the northern states hoping and wishing for a better life.

But run as she did, she never came to see us. I never even heard her voice after she moved away. The telephone wasn't in every household, and everybody was doing everything by telegraph or writing letters. I wasn't really concerned with knowing what my name meant or how she arrived at it at that time.

My father left town when I was just about one year of age. When I was old enough to understand why he wasn't around, I heard the story about the day my mother was standing in a bus line waiting to catch the bus from downtown back to Africatown, when a White man came up behind her, pulled her hair and said, "Nigger, why are you standing there in front of this White woman?" My dad was standing to the side, saw what was happening, and proceeded to beat him up. So he left town and never came back to live with us. His first stop was Cleveland, though he ended up in Chicago and died there about nine years ago.

Unlike my mother, he was part of my life in many ways. He used to send things and money back home. The first time I saw my father again I was 13. I was in the yard playing with my brother when I recognized him from the only photo we had of him when he was in the armed forces. Later on, when I was with the Mets, he came to all the games when we were in Chicago, and I always spent most of my time with him.

But my brother and I didn't know that our parents would never come home to stay after that, and we never gave it much thought. Our grandmother, Mama Myrt, became our caretaker and raised us all the way. Other kids around had broken families like ours, so after a while it felt pretty normal to us. But I never wanted that to feel normal to our children. I never wanted them to experience a mother not coming home, a father not coming home. I wanted them to experience what coming home means to me.

When my grandmother raised me and my brother, we lived in one house on the property and my great-grandmother lived in another. Our house was made of cypress wood with a tin roof, had four rooms and high ceilings, and I shared a room with my brother.

The school we attended was a block from our house. During those days our neighborhood was full of kids, maybe three or four thousand kids, so there never was a shortage of kids to play with or games to play. It wasn't unusual for families to have 10 kids or more—we had one family with 19 kids and another with 22. If you walked out onto the street with a baseball and threw it up, before it came down you had a team. And there were no parks.

We played on the middle school campus or the high school campus because the closest park to us was in Prichard, which was about three miles away.

We learned early on from Mama Myrt and from others in our community that being raised in the South at that time had its challenges for everybody who was Black. Living under the conditions of the Jim Crow laws that had been established right after Reconstruction ended in 1877 hampered people of color, and continued on until the Civil Rights Act of 1964 and the Voting Rights Act of 1965 had been passed into law. But there weren't any such laws protecting us when I grew up in the South, and I grew up in the Deep South, where some people were still fighting their own personal Civil War against us. Alabama wasn't the safest place on earth to be raised.

When we got old enough, the grownups taught us how to act at those times we'd be around White people. We'd been warned to do what we were told, because they'd had their experiences and knew what they were talking about. They told us to never get into a comfort zone and just to mind what we were doing and go on about our business. I did what they told us to do and encountered no troubles at all during my youth.

I'd never experienced any personal racism like my parents did growing up. I didn't know about all the prejudice and hatred going on outside of where we lived. I didn't know that just minding your own business could lead to trouble and we were better off mostly interacting with Black folks. It was just that way, being born and raised in Africatown. The only White folks we came in contact with were the insurance man, the police man, and other people selling products who would come by now and then. And I remember they were of good cheer when they had something they were trying to sell to us. And because I'd been shielded by the grownups around me, I mostly just played with my older brother and paid no attention to any problems that could be going on between the races.

I attended the first Black high school in Alabama, the Mobile County Training School (MCTS), as did my great-grandmother. During her time you would go as far as the fourth or fifth grade and then go to work. It was called a "training school" because you were being trained for whatever course of action you wanted to take. The word "training" certainly implied something but was not specific, and I never looked at it that way. To me, it was just another high school, and we'd produced a good number or doctors, lawyers, and other vocations like all the other high schools around had.

By 1960, about two-thirds of our high school graduates attended college. Some of them who went to college came back and got some decent jobs and made a good life for themselves. I was fortunate enough to fulfill a dream of mine by getting to the major leagues. There were definitely others who had those same aspirations, but many ended up working in the mills and other places.

People are still surprised when I tell them that I graduated from MCTS in 1961. Tommie Agee had graduated in 1960 and so did Billy Williams—and we had Hank Aaron and his brother Tommie, Willie McCovey, and Amos Otis as neighbors. I played sandlot ball with the two Tommies, Billy, and Amos, and heard stories from my elders about our greatest living legend at the time, Satchel Paige.

The Aaron brothers and Willie McCovey went to Central High School, which was our biggest rival in the city. They always had good teams and good athletes, and we all played baseball, football, basketball, and ran track. The schools were segregated with no interracial events except on Sunday, when we'd play against some of my White friends. Even though things were segregated, we got along well with each other and never sensed any racial strife or heard any racial comments from any of them.

We never got into any serious trouble—petty things like wrestling that sometimes led to fisticuffs that we forgot about when it was over. There was no stealing or harming folks and their property—Mama Myrt saw to that. Between the life lessons she taught us and reading to us from the Bible, we knew right from wrong and respected those around us. And if we ever did do something wrong, the neighborhood was like one big family—the word would spread, and you'd have to face the consequences.

I met my wife, Angela, when she was 14. I remember playing ball at Prichard Park, and I heard some people calling my name. I found out later she was one of those calling me, and we started talking to each other soon after. I didn't start going over to her house until much later when we got to know each other more. But when I started playing football, she became a majorette, and we got to see each other at the games.

After every game the girls would bring those big delicious red apples and give them to the player who deserved it most. If the guy ran for a touchdown, he'd get the most apples—I was running for four or five a game and would get the biggest share.

I believe my sharing with others began with those apples. There were players with no apples, and I'd have a bushel-full in front of me. I'd never gloat or hoard the bounty of apples but instead chose to share them with my teammates. It was a simple gesture and certainly the right thing to do—those messages from Mrs. McCants and Mama Myrt coming alive inside me. I could see for myself the joy on their faces to be on the receiving end, to have the star player of your team care enough to reach out and to share, and how that simple gesture brought even more respect and admiration.

But I never had any of that in mind. While I watched my teammates accept and enjoy whatever apples I gave them, I felt supreme satisfaction as the giver. There was a special joy in that, and I wanted more. I thought of what Mrs. McCants taught me, to "give back to society in ways that went far beyond money," and now I understood what she meant.

While I passed apples out to my teammates, I gave some extra apples to my friend, Bobby Knight, for safe-keeping until everyone left. Then I'd go around the neighborhood passing them out to other folks. When the bag was emptied and I headed home, I thought about the simplicity of sharing apples, the joyful expressions from my neighbors, and was grateful to be in that position of sharing.

Chapter 3

LEGENDS AND STARS

BASEBALL AND FOOTBALL were the predominant sports during the time I grew up, but baseball was the most popular in my community. I think some of that was because Blacks had started getting onto big-league teams, and most of us looked up to them and wanted to be like them.

I had decided early on that I wanted to be a baseball player because of Jackie Robinson and Larry Doby. I knew I could be, because of them. Before Jackie and Larry, you could play baseball but you could never see yourself being a major league ballplayer because there were no Blacks on any of the teams. Then after Jackie and Larry came players like Roy Campanella, Don Newcombe, and Joe Black. We already knew about Satchel Paige and Luke Easter and Sam Jones, and you could go on and on about them and others. Before all that, none of us dreamed of being a major league player. We might have thought about it, but we knew different.

I remember in my senior year in high school, we had to write an essay assigned by Ms. Blackman on how we envisioned our life and what we wanted to be. Even though I was being touted as probably the best football player in the state, my essay was about being like Jackie Robinson, Roy Campanella, Junior Gilliam, and Larry Doby. Even though they had yet to be in the Hall of Fame, I wrote that I wanted to be listed in the Hall of Fame with Willie Mays and Hank Aaron and Larry Doby and Jackie Robinson, players I thought for sure would one day be inducted. The teacher was impressed with that because nobody else came close to thinking that they could attain something like that. That was my motivation even to myself, not to dream, but to learn and believe that that's who I could be.

I played sandlot ball with guys who were great—maybe as great as Hank or Willie—but it wasn't until 1947 that Jackie broke the barrier. Unfortunately, a lot of those players never got the chance to showcase their talents in the major leagues. There have been so many great baseball players from the Mobile area, guys who were just fantastic—major-league-caliber players who never had a chance to get out of Mobile—even 40-year-old short-stops better than some of the pros I'd eventually see. I oftentimes think about them and can still see them in my mind's eye doing all the things a major league player can do and then some. Had Jackie come around even sooner, I'm sure we'd be talking about others from our area to go along with the likes of Henry Aaron, Tommie Aaron, Willie McCovey, Billy Williams, Tommie Agee, Amos Otis, myself, and of course, Satchel Paige.

Everybody in baseball knew who Satchel Paige was, and in the minds of many he was probably the best pitcher who ever lived. If you watch old film of Dizzy Dean talking about the great players of the game, he was always talking about the great Black players and that Satchel Paige was the greatest pitcher of them all.

By the time he made it to the major leagues, he was in his forties and had built a legendary status in the Mobile area. I was only 10 or 11 and just getting into playing myself when I started hearing some of the stories from the old guys about Satchel, stories that have circulated around here for decades and ones I never grow tired of telling because they are almost bigger than life. Now I'm one of those old guys who has a responsibility to tell those same stories in order to keep his legend alive, to remind the younger folks of how great he truly was and to pass such stories down, in person.

Ralph "Satch" Donahue was another star pitcher who told us stories about how he and Satchel Paige hooked up against one another at times, and everyone knew the game would be low-scoring or scoreless. I always tell this one story the way it was told to me by Ralph Donahue himself, and I never tire of telling it because of its legendary status in these parts. But it's been confirmed by others who were there that day. It confirms, to me, how great both men were when they took the mound, not only because of what they did when they started pitching but because of the type of players they were facing—guys who knew that their own name would reach some sort of celebrity status if they did well—especially against Satchel.

At one point during this particular game, Satchel Paige took the mound and told all of his players on the field to sit down at their positions because he was going to strike out the side. His players listened to him and then he did what he said he was going to to do and struck out the side. Well, that same inning when Ralph took the mound, he decided that if Satchel could do it, so could he, and had his players sit down at their positions. Ralph struck out the side, too. They pitched until dark at the old field they called the Ball Park, right here in Africatown.

If you were lucky enough to go to Black venues back then, like the barnstorming tours, it was a special treat. Most of the fields they played on didn't have the amenities of the White ballparks, and a lot of times they played in open fields that weren't really suitable for playing on, sometimes rocky and not always flat. Despite all that, when Satchel warmed up he didn't do it the normal way on the sideline. Often times they had no pitcher's rubber or home plate, so they measured out the distance from one to another and went from there. After the proper distance had been measured out, Satchel would place a bubble gum wrapper down around where home plate would be and have the catcher set up behind it. At that time he'd direct his catcher to give his target in and around the corners of that tiny piece of paper and would throw pitch after pitch in exactly those spots. He was that much of a perfectionist and that confident in his accuracy and abilities.

I remember coming up there was a team in almost every neighborhood. Magazine had a team. Africatown had a team. Prichard had a team, and there were others. All of the neighborhoods had their own team in the surrounding area, so we were entrenched in baseball, with football and basketball sidebars. Baseball was the natural thing for us to do because we had no real connection to basketball or football. Most basketball players were taller and football players were bigger. You could be tall, short, skinny, or overweight and still play baseball, and so everybody did.

The first real team I played on was called the Bumble Bees, when I was 12 years old. We put that team into Prichard Park just a mile or two from Africatown. It was the only park near us and the same one where Hank and Tommie Aaron played. There were no Black parks for us in our area, and mostly we played pickup games in the neighborhood and in the organized league at Prichard Park. We scrounged up some money and had our names put on T-shirts and got our own caps. We worked shining shoes and washing windows, cleaned yards just to get enough money to buy T-shirts or equipment. We wore sneakers and we had volunteer umpires, and plenty of folks came out to watch.

I was an accomplished player before I even owned my first glove. We used to share gloves when we were younger, and only a few of the guys were left-handed, so they always made sure we were always on opposite teams. I didn't own my own glove until I was 13 years old, and I didn't own any bats or balls, either. I was always playing with someone else's equipment, sharpening my skills with other people's gloves and bats. I got my first glove from my dad the first time he came home after leaving when I was just an infant. He came home from Chicago and brought me and my brother a glove, and I cherished it from that day on and kept it until I got to the big leagues.

When we got older, our manager was James Robinson, whom we called "Fat." He weighed over 300 pounds but was a gentle giant and had a heart of gold. He would make sure we had all the equipment, uniforms, and a field to play on. He always managed to get equipment for us so we could play and develop, and every day after work he set up a place for us to practice and play games on the weekends, so that's how we really developed into good ballplayers. The first bat I owned was a broken one given to me by James Robinson. I took it home and nailed it up good and taped it and thought I was on top of the world with my own glove, my own bat, and my own uniform.

Our uniforms came from the Mobile Bears semi-pro team—uniforms that they'd worn out and given to us. They may not have been perfect, but they were to us. They made us feel important and like big-league ballplayers. We got broken bats and fixed them up and did whatever it would take to be able to play ball.

I started out as a natural left-handed hitter, but that changed early on. When we were younger, we owned just one ball between the whole neighborhood, and where we were playing, right field was marshy and full of debris. I kept pulling the ball into the water in right field, and they said if I wanted to play anymore I had to learn to bat right-handed, so that gave me no choice. I proceeded to get on the other side and bat righty, and I became as good as when I batted lefty.

My brother was a good athlete. A good football player and a good track man, he was a pitcher and played second base. He was a good hitter at first but became gun-shy after being beaned by a pitch one day and then became afraid of the ball. He got hit a few more times after that and was more excited to play defense than bat. When he went to bat, he just wanted to get it over with and not get hit again, especially since we didn't even have batting helmets until later on.

Mobile has a rich history of baseball that goes back even before Satchel Paige. Even Babe Ruth and Lou Gehrig barnstormed through here early on. The city of Mobile—the whole region, actually—has been a home for baseball, especially for the Black man, because that was his real outlet, to try and master the game of baseball and hope that someday he'd be the one to break the major league color barrier.

Back in those days the Dodgers, Giants, and Braves would come through Mobile on their way back north after spring training, and they'd play exhibition games against our Mobile Bay Bears. I remember "The Rifleman" Chuck Connors and George "Shotgun" Shuba playing here. We had a chance to watch when Hank Aaron came to town, Willie Mays and Billy Bruton. Even Jackie Robinson came through a few times but never got close to my area. People would holler at Jackie, and he'd wave and come over, and that created a big stir.

We all collected baseball cards because we were baseball players, and even though we didn't have a television set to watch the games, we "watched" the games on the radio because we actually thought we could see what was going on. We all used to sit around these big radios and listen to the Brooklyn Dodgers or St. Louis, Chicago, or Cleveland games. I remember listening to Indians games because I really liked Larry Doby, and Dodgers games for Jackie. We'd sit there and listen to entire broadcasts—especially during the World Series—and I'd imagine myself one day playing in a World Series myself.

When I attended the Mobile County Training School with Tommie Agee, we played against city schools and county schools. Willie McCovey and Hank and Tommie Aaron attended rival Central High School. They always had good teams and good athletes. We were all close. Hank treated us like brothers. After he went pro, he came around and made a special effort to come over to talk and chat about home and the people we knew. He always asked about certain people we all knew and how they were doing. Family and friends were important to him and to all of us. Sure, we talked about baseball and the like, but when Hank came around, it was people first.

The first time I saw Hank I was in the seventh grade, and he'd already established himself as a star with the Milwaukee Braves. He came to the high school, and we had an assembly where he was the main speaker. Our principal, Mr. Hope, invited him to come so we could speak to and talk to a major league baseball player. I wasn't able to get close to him, but I tried. Everybody else was on the steps trying to get on the stage, so I didn't get a chance.

Hank and Willie McCovey were eight and four years ahead of us in school, so we never got to play against them. But when I was a rookie with the Mets, most of us got together during the spring and worked out together. There were no protective screens for the pitchers throwing batting practice, so we had to make sure the guys throwing to us would be safe—we didn't want them to be in harm's way. We decided we'd have to purposely take the ball to right or left field and hit nothing up the middle. There were always going to be guys like myself who didn't have that kind of bat control right off—I was just trying to hit the ball wherever I could. After a while I learned from watching the other guys how to channel where I wanted the ball to go. It served two purposes: we kept the guys safe on the mound, and we became more patient hitters.

When Billy Williams was dating his future wife, Shirley, he came home after the baseball season and came to Africatown, where Shirley lived just a couple blocks from me. He would see me often when I'd be fishing, and he'd stop and say, "Keep doing what you're doing, they're watching you." (He was referring to major league scouts.) He always had a kind word like that and always had time for people.

What I learned as a teenager about Willie McCovey was that they called him "Stretch" because he was 6'2" or 6'3" at that time and was very talented. I know in 1969, to me, he might have been the best hitter in baseball and had been a force for the Giants along with Willie Mays. During my years with the Mets, before each game we had team meetings and talked about how to pitch to and line up defensively against guys throughout the opposing lineup. Everybody had the same concept for pitching to McCovey—you had to throw a fastball up because he had problems getting to it. Down and in and down and away, he was great at hitting those. In 1969 that all changed, we just didn't know how to pitch him.

I remember when I first got to the Mets, Casey Stengel went over the hitters of the opposing team and when we arrived at guys like McCovey, Casey would say, "Skip him, we don't have anybody can get him out," and we just went to the next guy. We did that with all the good hitters—so many good hitters in the league at that time. We had no cure for Hank Aaron or Billy Williams or Willie McCovey until we started to get guys like Seaver, Koosman, and Ryan, and even then we learned that the good hitters are going to get theirs, anyway, you just have to limit everybody else.

McCovey—and I hate to say this—never wanted to come back home to Mobile. We had a McCovey Day for him once, and I had to talk him into coming back and promised I'd be with him just about every second he was here. He had bad memories of things that took place here in Mobile that he never wanted to talk about. Even though he had family here, he was never motivated to come back home.

But I've learned that people are people everywhere, and that memories can play tricks on you. I always tell people that circumstances are the way they are because of the position you were in at that particular time, and if you can't forgive—I'm not saying forget—if you can't forgive a circumstance, how can you heal and move forward? He wasn't willing to do that because of his bad experiences. He had a lot of friends he played with and against in Mobile, and when we talked he always talked about them and mentioned them, but I never got out of him what happened or when or how it happened—and why it was traumatizing him enough that he wasn't willing to set it aside and to grow and move forward.

I was lucky that I was given all kinds of encouragement growing up.

I was told all the time I had all the tools to be a professional athlete, especially a baseball player. The people who inspired me were people who were older, many of whom had great baseball talent but were born too far before things started to change for the Black baseball player. Listening to people talk about Satchel Paige and other local greats encouraged me to become like them. They gave you a platform to work, and it became up to you to take it as far as you could.

So, yes, it was my neighborhood that planted a seed and cultivated it in me to become a major league ballplayer. In that context, I owe all of that to my neighborhood. It could have been just the opposite, with nobody paying any attention or letting me use their equipment. It could have been different if nobody had put forth the effort to speak to me and tell me to keep doing what I was doing because it might have a tremendous outcome. My success wasn't really my success. I recognized that right away and always knew I would always come back home to my neighborhood when I was needing encouragement or motivation when things were tough. I didn't want to let all those people down who had helped me achieve my dream to play in the majors.

Chapter 4

THE CONTRACT

I WAS A FOUR-SEASON man when I attended high school, and I excelled in all of them. From football to baseball, track to basketball, I played them all. I was told during my high school career that I could be a professional football player, that my strength was football.

Charles Rhodes was my head football coach, and he was influential, as Mrs. McCants was. He was like a rock and had everybody's attention even if he wasn't speaking. When he did speak, everybody listened and everybody always responded to his commands. We had other coaches, like Coach Hardin, Coach Washington, and Coach Jackson—all good people, but they didn't command respect like coach Rhodes.

When I was a freshman, I got hit hard in a game and tore up my knee—the very knee that would trouble me in baseball years later. I was hurt so badly I couldn't practice for weeks, and Coach Rhodes wanted to take me and another injured player—Willie Matthews—off the roster to be replaced by two other guys. But we were better athletes. I told him I was on the team and was staying on the roster.

He dropped Willie off the team and put a couple guys on the roster but kept me on. I didn't get a chance to play again that year, but he admired the fact that I wouldn't quit. I told him he was going to see this again, that I'm going to pay him back for trying to cut me. He said, "What do you mean?" And I said, "You'll see someday."

When I got to be a senior, I was the star of the team and I was on everybody's tongue and mind as an elite talent from the surrounding area. When we got ready to go on our bus for an away game, I told the guys I was going to have Coach wait for me, that I'd be around the corner watching the bus out of his sight and that this was my payback from when I was a freshman. The rest of the guys boarded the bus, and I could see for myself Coach was looking for me, and I heard him ask the guys, "Where is he? Where is he?" over and over. Everybody acted like they didn't know where I was, and he kept carrying on, saying I knew like everyone else when we were supposed to be there and when we were supposed to leave. I heard him say he'd give me 10 minutes more and then would leave without me.

I waited right up until the end and walked up to the bus where he was standing, and he said, "Where you been?" I said, "What did I tell you, Coach? I told you I was gonna pay you back." He started laughing and said that I was never late before, he was just concerned. That was me with that little mean streak inside that came out every now and then.

But my love was always baseball simply because of the history of it. Jackie Robinson and Larry Doby gave my grandparents so much pleasure when they listened to the games on the radio. For all of us to know that major league baseball was being transformed for Blacks gave us more of a connection. We already had love for the game because Blacks gravitated to baseball. But Babe Ruth, Joe DiMaggio, Ted Williams, and all those people before Jackie got in the game, they were our heroes because of our love of the game.

But my focus was primarily on football at the time because the community gravitated around football and the pride it gave the community based on how well your high school did in the city and in the county. My school always had good teams and great athletes who set the standards for football. I was lucky enough to break all the records running the football. We played eight or nine games each year before there were statewide play-offs, but we played in the city championship and won practically every year. I think we lost one game each year, and thinking back on it, with the team we had and the coaching we had, I don't know how we managed that.

When I came up to high school, the school record was 16 touchdowns. I ended up with 26 and could have run 50 more that year, but whenever we got close to the goal line, Coach wanted others who hadn't scored to score. I never got any short touchdowns of one or two yards, even 10 yards.

Most of mine were from 95 yards—long runs, that kind of thing.

Of course, everything was segregated, so we didn't have the chance to play the White schools. That didn't stop the White kids from coming to watch us play, and it didn't stop the college scouts, either. I remember getting offers from Minnesota, Illinois, all the Black schools, and letters from other White schools. As much as I was being watched, my heart was always on baseball, so I ended up accepting a scholarship from Grambling.

I visited Coach Eddie Robinson and enrolled in Grambling in August 1961 to play both football and baseball. I practiced with the football team a few times, but I wasn't sure I chose the right school. So many guys from my neighborhood went to Alabama A&M, and they kept writing me and telling me I needed to be at A&M with them. After a while I started to believe it. I was feeling homesick and really missed Angela. That's when I told Coach that I wanted to go home to see her.

Robinson—Coach "Rob"—was mild-mannered and a great motivator and more than what I thought he was. He was a great man, thoughtful and considerate, tutoring many fine athletes in their studies. You would never know his accomplishments unless you sat down and talked with him because he was so humble. He could talk the horns off a mountain goat, but he was wise and understanding and gave me a round-trip bus ticket home. Coach thought for sure I'd be back, but I was torn and wasn't sure about the immediate future.

It was during that bus ride home that I had time to think things over and to decide what was really best for me. I had a full scholarship and was playing for the best Black coach and team in the country. I would have been a key player for them, and likely the pro teams would've noticed me. As much as I was comfortable at home and always was, transferring to A&M was still about the same 350 miles from home as Grambling was, so there was no advantage in that. So I contemplated the whole thing, and as hard as it might have been, I made up my mind I wasn't going back to Grambling and would enroll at A&M instead.

At that time A&M didn't have a scholarship program, but they managed somehow to get one for me. By the time I got settled in, the football season was about to begin, so I had to watch the season opener from the sideline. I couldn't help but compare what they had to what Grambling had. They had a good team, but they were no Grambling. Grambling had 14–15 pro prospects on their roster, and A&M might have had one other than me.

My first game was against Fisk, and I think I scored three or four touchdowns. Coach Robinson was in Tennessee to play Tennessee State, and I didn't know he was at our game. He'd brought the whole team down to watch me play. After the game he came down to the field with a couple coaches, shook my hand, and told me he'd be having a whole conversation to his team in what he saw me do in our game. Most of the guys came around and shook my hand and started calling me "Beep-Beep" after the Roadrunner.

I played well at A&M and started getting letters from the Cleveland Browns and other teams even as a freshman, but I was focused on playing baseball. When the baseball season started, I came home for the weekend, and that's when I had a life-changing event that almost killed me and changed my thinking for good about needing to stick with baseball and forget football.

I was sitting in a car talking to a friend no more than a block from home when some guy came barreling down the street and hit us head-on. I went through the windshield, just lying on the hood not really knowing what just happened until people started crying and yelling for help. That told me I was in pretty bad shape, but I was comfortable the whole time, even when the ambulance took me down to the hospital and began trying to sew me up. It was only when I heard our friend William Robinson asking the doctors if I was going to make it that I knew I was in trouble. And he kept asking, "Is he gonna make it, is he gonna make it?"

For the first time that thought went to my head that I was really, really hurt. I couldn't see the position I was in and for some reason I never felt the pain when it happened and still didn't. I didn't know if I'd lost an eye or if I still had the eye or if I'd lost my vision because my eyelid had been slit and covered my eye.

It turns out the doctors were able to stop the bleeding and save my eye with no damage to it, though the glass left a permanent scar on the right side of my face. But I was alive and thankful to be because I didn't know if I was going to live or die. It took weeks for me to recover.

The accident changed everything for me, and that's when I decided that I was done with football for good and needed to concentrate strictly on baseball. When you go through that kind of ordeal, the first thing people want to know is are you fit, did you damage something that will impede you progress, questions like that. That got me thinking of how demanding and physical football was and how any injury at any time could end a career. I'd had my share of football injuries at the high school level and knew firsthand how injuries stay with you. While I was young enough and strong enough to recover, going through that windshield was a game-changer.

Years later, when my knee started bothering me, I knew it was from the old football injuries during high school when I played just about every snap of every game on offense, defense, and special teams. Taking hit after hit or hitting someone else takes its toll on a body. But I was too young and eager to know better and wanted to be in on the action.

In the previous summer, my friend and neighbor, Tommie Agee, signed with the Cleveland Indians for about $60,000. I always thought I was a better player than him, and so did everybody else around. I was hoping for the same kind of deal, but what I really wanted was the chance to play.

A few scouts like George Crow and Ed Scott took a look at me when I was playing for the Mobile Black Bears semi-pro team. Then four or five teams showed some interest, but nobody gave me any offers. That's when a good friend of mine by the name of Clyde Gray got involved as sort of agent. Clyde told me I was good enough to play in the major leagues, that he'd seen all of them, but nobody could do what I could do. He said he was going to write to the Mets because they had a new organization and he thought they should come down and have a look at me. They responded and sent Julius Morgan down to watch me play.

I remember in my only at-bat I hit a home run before the rains came. Julius wanted to see more and talked to us about driving to Atlanta and onto Salisbury for a workout where the Mets had a little co-op team.

Clyde drove me to Atlanta then on to Salisbury, where I worked out with about 30 other guys and then by myself. I responded well enough to impress Morgan, and he offered me a $10,000 contract on the spot. I said. "No, that's not enough money. You'll have to give me more than that, and if you don't, I'm going back home."

He said, "Look. I can give you $10,000 right here on the spot but nothing even close to Tommie Agee type money." He paused and said, "I'll tell you what, I got this country boy living in the next town, and they say he can throw as hard as a mule can kick. I'm gonna go get him, and if you can hit him, they'll probably give you the money you want."

I said, "Go over and get him."

The next morning he came back, and I asked where the guy was. He said he went into the Army and wasn't around anymore. That's when he said I'd have to go to New York to hit off of some of the Mets pitchers like Al Jackson.

I stuck to my convictions and left with Clyde, wanting to think things over. On the way home, Clyde reminded me I might not get the money I was after, but probably could get more than $10,000. But he said this was my opportunity and probably the best organization to move up quickly in. Everything he said made sense to me.

When we got back home, Julius Morgan was sitting on the porch talking to my grandmother. When I got out of the car Mama Myrt said, "Boy, come here. This nice White man trying to give you all this money, and you're acting the fool. Come here. Give me those papers, mister. Boy, get somewhere to sit down and sign this man's papers."

Well, there was no talking back to Mama Myrt. That's how I ended up signing with the Mets. It was the best move I ever made and the best thing Clyde Gray ever did for me.

You know, it wasn't $60,000, but it was a lot of money for us. We had never seen that kind of money before, and she just thought I was being stupid to turn it down. There was an opportunity, and she thought I was being foolish. She didn't know I was fighting for more because I thought I was worth more and I could get more. Like always, Mama Myrt was right, and I didn't debate that at all.

When I got the money, we put it in the bank, and I kept about $200. My goal was to build a house. When I went to winter ball, I remember going to First National Bank with that check. The guy at the bank who waited on us was a big baseball fan, and he sparked my ego.

If I had to do it all over again, I'd still sign that contract because it was an opportunity to go with an organization that turned out to be first-class. I rose through the organization pretty quickly after that.

Chapter 5

THE RACISM (1962)

AFTER SIGNING WITH the Mets in 1962, they sent me to the Florida Instructional League in Pensacola, where other young players and I would be instructed for about a month on the mechanics of throwing, running, hitting, and defense. I wasn't sure what to expect, and it was certainly a learning experience. It was also the first time I got to meet some of the original Mets.

When I first met Ed Kranepool, he was already a polished player. He knew the strike zone well. He didn't swing at bad pitches. He was a good fielder at first base. He did everything right. He looked like a bonus baby. When I talked to the scouts about signing, I heard that Eddie got somewhere between $80,000 and $100,000, and there wasn't much left for me.

Ed Kranepool deserved every penny he got with whatever signing bonus it was. He never became the player that everybody hoped he would be because he didn't hit home runs like they thought he would. But he was an everyday player and to me a great talent. On most lineups he would have been an everyday first baseman, and he was, before Donn Clendenon arrived in 1969. And to play all your career for one team was a hard thing to do, especially considering trades and when free-agency came about, but Ed did that for 18 years.

Al Jackson was a stabilizer in the Mets organization as I see it. As a matter of fact, he helped me immensely to understand the game, the people in the game, and to encourage me that I could play in the big leagues, that I was a big-league talent. He stressed that, as a professional athlete, the right attitude is essential. If you don't believe in yourself and what you can do, then chances are you can't do it. He talked baseball with me a lot, and the Mets were smart enough to put me with him on the road later on. Not only that, they were smart enough to put my wife, Angela, with his wonderful wife, Nadine, where she could learn from her.

My roommate for that month was Paul Blair. He was a funny guy, who didn't mind talking about himself. I could see he was a talented player, but the Mets didn't protect him in the draft right after the Instructional League ended. That surprised me because they were looking for young players and won just 40 games their first year. The Mets had an older outfield with guys like Richie Ashburn, Frank Thomas, Gene Woodling, and Gus Bell. Blair was fast and quick. When Ashburn retired, Duke Snider came over the nest season, but he was past his prime.

I'll never know to this day why he wasn't protected, because he clearly showed he was a major league prospect. Had the Mets kept him before Baltimore found him, and had they drafted Reggie Jackson instead of Steve Chilcott with the No. 1 pick in 1966, that Mets outfield could have been Cleon Jones, Paul Blair, and Reggie Jackson. That didn't happen, and it's fun to think about if it did. If it had happened, it would have made all of us better because we would have had that kind of competition where we could have competed with each other. It would have made the team better.

I looked at Cincinnati and Pittsburgh with all those good hitters, and each of them made the other one better. I would have loved to have had something like that with the Mets because it would have made me better. Good hitters make other hitters better. Think about what Eddie Kranepool could have been as a young hitter if he'd had talent like that around him in the lineup. He was an island by himself, because most of the time when he came up to bat, nobody was on base. Pitchers can take chances and pitch you the way they want to. When somebody's on base or in scoring position, it puts you in the driver's seat. You'll get better pitches to hit, especially if somebody's behind you who can hit like a Reggie Jackson or a Paul Blair. It's no secret how and why Roger Maris hit 61 home runs batting in front of Mickey Mantle in 1961.

I'm not saying that's the reason why the Mets struggled again in 1963, but it may have been one of them. I talked with Paul during the 1969 World Series about just that. We'd been hoping to be teammates for a long time, and now one of us was going to win the World Series. Of course, he told me he already had a ring when the Orioles swept the Dodgers just at few years earlier. And look what happened after that—another ring with the Orioles and later two more with the Yankees where he played, ironically, with Reggie Jackson.

I shared an apartment near the ballpark with Paul for that month, away from the White players. The ballclub had to segregate the White players from the Black players—even though it had been years since Jackie Robinson and every club from both leagues had Black players on their rosters. Even the big club had to get apartments for the Black players, and we had to take a taxi to the ballpark every day.

There had so much unrest around the country that year, and it would get worse later on. Blacks standing up against authority, hoping for change and equality, even risking their own lives to attain something that was our right. Of course we had Martin Luther King Jr., Ralph Abernathy, and Jesse Jackson fighting the fight, and even Rosa Parks had stood up against the rules. But there were others like Dion Diamond, Bob Moses, Reggie Robinson, and Bill Hansen who weren't the big names everybody came to know, but they were strong-minded individuals who had that mindset and the will to do the right thing for their brothers and sisters.

Segregation had its ugly head high and wide, so we realized what we were up against and abided by the situation at that time until things got better. We were in no position to take a stand at the time. You spend your life trying to have an opportunity to play on the same fields as Jackie, Larry Doby, Roy Campanella, and Joe Black. Everything was segregated at that time, and you knew there was a small window of opportunity when you could squeeze through it and take a stand. That opportunity just hadn't presented itself yet. That would all change when I went to play at Auburn in 1963 in the New York–Penn League, when the racism I encountered didn't come from the good people of Auburn, but from our manager.

I had such a bad case of hemorrhoids I could hardly walk, let alone play ball. I was living upstairs over a bar-restaurant, and when I was in bed the vibrations from the music in the bar were just killing me. It was that bad. I decided to tell our manager how I was feeling and went to the ballpark the next day with that intention.

When I got to the ballpark I told him my situation and that I needed to go home and have surgery. Well, the Mets had tried to get me to have surgery earlier in New York, but I told them I wouldn't have it there, I'd rather have it at home so I could be with my grandmother who could look after me.

So I told him the situation, and he just ignored what I said. He said he was going to put me in the lineup until he heard more about it from New York, and until such time, I was playing. I told him with more urgency in my voice that I couldn't play, that I could hardly walk and certainly couldn't run. But he ignored what I had to say and put me in the lineup anyway.

I was hitting around .360 and could tell already I was the team's best hitter, and that's what the manager knew as well. I know he wanted my bat in the lineup and my speed and defense, but he was stubborn and paid no mind to what I had I say.

I played that night, and I was right. I could hardly run in or out to center field or even to first base. The pain kept getting worse inning by inning, and I knew he wouldn't take me out of the game if I complained at all, so I kept playing. I was sure I had irritated my injury and was concerned it probably would set me back further. I struggled to finish that game, but I did. And as I thought about the conditions he'd set for me, I thought long and hard about what my next move would be. I knew I couldn't play another inning, let alone a whole game, until I had the surgery. But I knew the stubborn mindset of the manager and knew he'd put me in the lineup the next night. He was stone-cold about the whole thing and never asked me during or after the game how I was feeling. Just about anybody could tell I was struggling, but that didn't seem to matter to him. He was in charge and what he said was final. It was really that simple. That's when I decided I'd made my mind up and was going to go back home to have the surgery. That night I packed up my stuff and caught a bus to Mobile.

Everybody started saying I ran off, and didn't know why I did it the way I did. There's always someone who could tell you it could have been handled differently, but I didn't see another way to handle it. I didn't see this guy sitting down with me, telling me he could feel my pain, and we needed to do something about it. I didn't feel that at all, so I took matters into my own hands.

But the Mets' Johnny Murphy, who was assistant general manager at that time, said they actually knew my situation. So they sent somebody down to check on me and found that I'd already been admitted to the hospital and was preparing for surgery. So I had the surgery and the Mets paid for it, and that's when I really was confronted for the first time in my life about racism in the world of the Black man from the eyes of the White man.

From that time forward, I realized that what was on the table for the White man wasn't on the table for the Black man. If you didn't have a broken bone or couldn't throw or had a leg injury where you couldn't walk or run, they didn't pay any attention to that. They couldn't feel your pain. I played with White boys who essentially couldn't play because of a broken fingernail, and it was excused. This manager was cold as ice.

Some things you have control of, some things you do not. You know, the situation in Auburn, I had no control over. I was just following orders—not that I was in the service—but trying to be the good guy and do the right thing because I'd been told to do something by the manager. But, by being in the lineup, I knew it could hurt the team and do more damage to myself. When I left the ballpark, things would then be in my hands. I could take control of it, never realizing the consequences of what the manager might say to the Mets front-office people. I don't know everything he said even up this day, only that he said some things that he didn't need to say, like I was lazy and selfish. That was really the first time I was confronted about racism in the eyes of a White man. That's when you realize how it all works.

Being from the South, of course I knew all about segregation and racism. I knew about all these things. But the first time I really got confronted with it was a wakeup call. I'd participated in sit-ins and demonstrations before—those kinds of things— and been spit on and called all kinds of names that served to toughen me up.

It may be hard to believe this was my first major issue with racism, but you have to realize that I came from Africatown, and that my interactions were mostly with Black folks, and we got along fine with each other for the most part. Sure, there was the insurance man, the police man, other people selling products that came, but they were of good cheer. The White vendors were talking and smiling, trying to make a sale. I saw that, but I knew that if I got outside of my comfort zone, there could be consequences, like what happened to my dad.

All this happened in late April and carried over into the first part of May as I recovered. I stayed home during that time and then got a call from the Mets telling me they wanted me to go to Raleigh to play in the Carolina League, and that was fine by me. My doctor had given me a timetable when he thought I could get back on the field, so I went to Raleigh under the impression that I wouldn't be playing for a few weeks. By the time I arrived in Raleigh, I hadn't picked up a ball or swung a bat for several weeks.

When I got there, the club was on the road for a few more days, and when they came back home the manager, Clyde McCullough, took me into his office to talk about my situation. Apparently he hadn't yet read the doctor's report or been told about it because he wanted to know if I could play right away. I was somewhat surprised and told him the doctor had set a timetable for seven to 10 days before I could return to the field. I told him I wasn't completely healed and still needed some time before taking the field.

I'd been in the Instructional League with McCullough and in Winter Ball a few months before that with his assistant coach, Solly Hemus. They were my first managers and knew me, and he knew what I could do. McCullough was one of the good guys I'd played for, so of course I wanted to play for him, but knew I shouldn't rush things. He listened to what I was saying but went on to say they had a doubleheader that night and asked me again, this time with more urgency in his voice, if I could play that night. I told him again that the doctor had said 10 days before I could play, but he didn't let up, saying again he had a double-header today and that I could play on one leg better than the guys he had there. So he asked me once more if I could play just one game. I finally gave in and said I would.

I played the one game, and I think we won and I got a few hits. And my body seemed to be doing fine, just a little pain but bearable. So he put me in the lineup for the second game. My adrenaline took over, I guess, the excitement of playing again and I kind of forgot about my situation by then. So I played in both games. He even ended up giving me the steal sign at some point in the game. I stayed in the lineup after that every day, but I had to go home every night and soak. I was feeling like a whole person again being back on the field and playing for someone who appreciated me.

My wife-to-be and her mother decided to visit me a few days later, but when they came out to the ballpark they were told they had to sit down the third-base line to watch the game with the other Black fans. It was a segregated area that most ballparks in the South still had back then, and despite their relationship to me, they were told it was the only place in the ballpark they were allowed to watch the game from.

I didn't want to be part a team that had those kinds of restrictions. The experience I'd had with the manager in Auburn was fresh in my mind, and I would have none of it again. That's when I told them that, if my girlfriend and her mother couldn't sit behind home plate, I wouldn't play.

It was times like those when I realized that it was my turn to stand up for what was right, that I couldn't just be grateful for Jackie Robinson with words, but had to back that up with deeds, and be prudent when I did. I thought about Jackie and what he might have done here, and knew whatever decision he would've made would be final. He wouldn't back down or give in or turn back. He'd take it all the way.

When those words, *turn back*, came to mind, I realized it wasn't just Jackie who was in me, it was my ancestors and others who'd been illegally taken from their African homeland before the start of the Civil War and settled in the Mobile area, and that I was, in some way, representing them, too.

I was just a boy when I learned about all that, and that was when this sense of community I carry first took root. We used to sit around the table with our elders and they'd tell their stories about the *Clotilda*—a ship nearly 100 feet long that was packed with over 100 enslaved people. It was also when I found out our family was from that North African contingency, people entrenched in the area well before the *Clotilda* landed here.

As those conversations started and continued on at other times, I became interested in where they all came from, why it had happened, who they were, who brought them over, and the many hardships they'd endured on a nearly two-month voyage across the ocean. At times I'd go to bed and conjure up images of the *Clotilda* and its captives, trying to imagine a 100-foot ship, the storms they went through, what it felt like to be bound and chained naked, not knowing where you were going, not knowing the language or if you were going to be cast overboard.

I remember them saying that some folks thought the saga of the *Clotilda* was nothing more than a myth, a story made up for some reason or other because they'd been searching 100 years for it. My grandparents and great-grandmother used to say the *Clotilda* sank or was burned, but either way, it still hadn't been located. I heard them say the passengers were transported from the *Clotilda* to a paddle-boat or steamship and transported north right at the start of the Civil War, and they stayed there until the war ended when Timothy Meaher—the owner of the boat—had to release them to get rid of any evidence that there was a voyage. Then he split the cargo of passengers up, brought some to Mobile, while others went inland to other counties and started to hide out for a while, then helped build our community along with other Blacks who'd been here already.

They weren't bothered by Meaher because both he and the boat's captain were under suspicion by the federal government for piracy. While they went looking for evidence, Meaher gave them jobs and sold them land to try and make the authorities look the other way. Even with all those folks from the *Clotilda* in our area, they never put two and two together, and Meaher never got into trouble.

They'd been searching for the *Clotilda* all of my life and about 80 years before that. As the years went on, some folks started giving up on the idea or just forgot about it, but I never did. It had always been important to me that we find some evidence. And even though they said the ship was burned to cover up the evidence, some artifacts or parts of the ship would still be there, somewhere in the river.

When I was younger and formed an interest in the story, I was able to talk with some of the children of the people who came over on that ship and who lived just a couple doors away. My dad's best friend was the grandson of Cudjoe Lewis—one of the last known survivors from the *Clotilda*—and he had two sisters, Mary and Martha. The stories they told were second-hand, but to me, they were as good as first-hand because they came from the mouths of the people who'd been told stories by those on that ship.

Cudjoe Lewis wasn't his real name, he was born Oluale Kossola, changed it to Kazoola and finally to Lewis. He died in 1935 but by then had shared his life stories with the girls. I latched onto every word they spoke, from the culture of the people to how it was they were taken. They said they'd come from a tribe about 100 miles inland in West Africa called the Tarkars, a peaceful people who farmed the land. There was no formalized religion or place of worship, but they did believe in a version of heaven and hell and lived honestly at all times. I'd had images of Africa where animals ran free and tribes of people were at war, so I was surprised at this. But when they kept talking and started to tell us more, those images I had were on target.

One day a scouting party of Dahomeyans showed up and made some demands, but the Tarkars refused. A few weeks later an entire army from Dahomey attacked the village and beheaded the young and the elderly. The remaining survivors were chained together and marched to the coast, then sold to Captain William Foster—the master of the *Clotilda*. That's when their voyage began.

All that was in me when I took a stand for Angela and her mother, and I wouldn't back down. One thing led to another, and some people got upset with what I was asking for. After a while, when they could tell I was serious about the matter, the general manager stepped in and let Angela and her mother sit behind home plate to watch the game.

As it turned out, it was a great move for everybody. And it didn't cause any problems. It was kind of a feeling of just letting folks—both Black and White—watch some baseball together and not look at colors. It wasn't about what was going on outside the ballpark, or anybody making a big deal over what I'd requested. It was all about what was going on inside the ballpark. It was nice to see that together they were pulling for the same team and had the same love and emotion for the game, and that's what took over.

The following night I told these two Black guys who were always at the games to join the ladies behind home plate, and without a problem or any confrontation they did. One of the guys everybody called "Iron Mike" was really entertaining everybody behind home plate. They gave him that nickname because you could hear his booming voice all around the entire ballpark. He had a saying, "Hey you rally caps! Bring out the caps and bring out the cannons!" He was a real baseball fan, he just loved the game. And six years later in 1969 I saw him when we were traveling north from spring training with the Mets for an exhibition game with Baltimore in Durham. He was in the ballpark—you could hear him clear as day. And I went over and talked to him because he was waving at me and calling my name.

It never crossed my mind about any possible repercussions from my actions. There was nothing written about what happened in the papers the next day. The only thing I was thinking about is, why should my future wife and mother-in-law sit in the hog pen when they can sit at the dinner table and enjoy the meal much better? It showed me that if you wanted something to change—and change for the better—you had to take matters into your own hands just like I did when I went home for the operation. I would have that mindset at all times.

The women went to a few of our away games while they were still visiting, and I didn't raise Cain on those away games, so they sat down the right-field line with the other Black folks. I didn't do or say anything about that because I was just concerned about my home park and where I played, and that there should be some consideration for the players' families. Making that one needed change made me feel good about the team and the management. And I knew I had the power inside to stay strong and stick to what I believed was right.

Chapter 6

CASEY

AT THE END of our 1963 minor league season I had played in just 63 games between Auburn and Raleigh but put up some decent numbers. My goal from the very start was to be a .300 hitter, and I'd done that for both teams. It was a small sampling of what I knew I was capable of doing and gave me confidence going forward, because the results were what I had wanted.

You come into a new organization wanting to make an impression, but you never know how good your teammates are, or your competitors. You think about all the games you played back home against your peers and then what you've learned and seen in the Instructional League, and you start to get the answers. I never questioned what I could do on the field and just wanted to move up as fast as I could. I knew I was in the best organization for something like that to happen.

When the Mets called me up in late September, it was the first time I'd ever seen a major league ballpark. I'd been to Hartwell Field back in Mobile, when the Dodgers barnstormed there on their way north following spring training, and was in awe seeing Jackie Robinson, even from a distance. Teams used to do that, and they'd stop off at one of their farm teams and play an exhibition game, then move on north to open the season. I even got to see Hank Aaron play there, and years before that, Babe Ruth and Lou Gehrig came through with the Yankees. It was a big mistake when they tore it down in 1979. But walking onto the Polo Grounds in 1963 was a whole other feeling altogether.

I knew beforehand that the dimensions of the field were oddly shaped and good for both right-handed and left-handed pull hitters—and I mean right down-the-line pull hitters. Now I could see for myself how far the home run hit by Bobby Thomson against the Dodgers in that 1951 playoff game needed to travel. If he had been just a fraction of a second late with his swing, it might have been a double or an out, which might have changed the results of that game.

But once you got into the gaps, the whole thing changed drastically and became 450' before you knew it. Dead center was right around where the clubhouse was, and the guys used to say it was a five-dollar taxi ride from there to the dugout.

I got my first chance to play in that outfield when Casey sent me into center for defense in the ninth inning of a game against Houston. There were probably 5,000 fans to start the game, but by then it had started to empty out and almost felt empty standing in that cavernous center field with probably 150' feet of open ground behind me and to either side. I looked at Ed Kranepool in left and Duke Snider in right—neither one of them known for his speed—and knew anything hit into either gap would be mine, though that was expected for a center fielder. It got me to thinking about Willie Mays making that catch against the Indians' Vic Wertz in the 1954 World Series and how far he'd had to run to get it. Now that I was standing where Willie once stood, I had a new level of respect for him as an outfielder.

I didn't have any action during that inning, but Bob Aspromonte hit a long home run over Eddie's head in left. When the inning ended, I ran in from center hoping for a chance to get my first major league at-bat, even though I was scheduled to bat eighth in the inning. Jim Hickman, "Hot" Rod Kanehl, and

Frank Thomas went down in order, and we were shut out—our 100th loss of the season, which kept us in last place, seven games behind our expansion rivals from Houston.

The next day Casey penciled me in as the leadoff hitter, and of course I wanted to make an impression. I made my first outfield catch in the first inning off the bat of John Weekly, but grounded out to the pitcher leading off the bottom of the inning. Then I did it again in the third. With two men on in the fifth, I thought I'd have another chance, but Casey sent Duke Snider in to pinch-hit for me.

I found out later from the guys that Casey had been known to do such things and would even pinch-hit for you in the first inning sometimes. It was always something like that going on with Casey. Guys who were in the on-deck circle never knew if he was going to pinch-hit for them, because he had this thing about certain guys hitting against certain pitchers. He had that kind of a talent way before all these new analytics today, and he remembered those kinds of things without writing it down or needing any notes to look at. When I played for him he was 75 years old and still had a great mind for the game. He made some statements in team meetings and things about players, and you wondered how he knew all those things.

Casey had a way with umpires and writers. Everybody had a delightful time being around him, whether it was before or after the game, because he always was hilarious in the way he commanded a crowd and how he talked—even to the umpires.

In one of our games, our starting pitcher got into trouble, and at that time we didn't have a good pitching staff for Casey to choose from. Casey went out to make a pitching change, and like most players or managers, he jumped over the white line after coming out of the dugout and his right arm went up a bit. When Casey got to the mound, waiting for the relief pitcher to come in, he didn't know the umpires thought he'd signaled for a right-hander after his hand went up.

Casey started talking to the umpires, but when he saw who was coming in from the bullpen, he looked around and said to the umpires, "That's not the guy I wanted, I wanted my lefty." He kept saying he didn't raise his hand, and the umpires said that he did and because he was on his way to the mound, they couldn't change it. Casey kept at it, "I don't want him. I want the left-hander, he's the one I want!" That went on for a while, but the umpires wouldn't back down, so the right-hander came into the game and actually did a good job.

The next day the umpire who had called the pitcher in was now the home-plate umpire. He looked at the lineup like they always did to make sure there were no mistakes and said to Casey, "Casey, take a look at the lineup," but Casey sort of ignored him and was talking to the other umpires. He said again, "Casey. Take a look at the lineup," but Casey kept on talking, and then the umpire in a more firm voice said, "Casey, you need to look at the lineup, you've made a mistake." And Casey looked up at him and said, "What's the problem?" The umpire said, "You don't have a pitcher on here." And Casey said, "You did such a fantastic job picking him yesterday, how about you pick another one today?"

Casey was a Hall of Fame manager and probably the most entertaining manager who ever managed in baseball. The writers loved him because he could talk and entertain after the ballgame late into the night, and they never grew tired of it. He had a sense about what people liked and how to give it to them. Even though he had bad teams, he always gave the reporters what they wanted so they could write a good story about it.

He had a story for every event. He had a story for every game. He had a story for every player. Casey had some great teams with the Yankees, and even though he was 75 years old, his memory was sharp. He could remember what every ballplayer did and what he was good at. It didn't matter what league he was in, he could converse on that player. It was little things he said with the team. He just had a way of being in control. Nobody doubted him, even when he did send guys up to the plate as a pinch-hitter in the first inning.

Then I went 0-for-4 against Philadelphia with another groundout to the pitcher—my third in just a few at-bats. Casey kept me in the game, but I must have been trying to do too much and never hit the ball out of the infield. I was 0-for-6 to that point and decided to start really paying attention to how the guys went about their business before, during, and after the games. Some of the veterans like Duke Snider and Frank Thomas might skip batting practice some days, and judging by their ages and the fact they both played the outfield, I felt there was going to be some opening for some playing time in the near future for me. But I had to show them more than what they'd been seeing.

We'd split the first two games of the three-game series against the Giants in San Francisco. Willie McCovey hit two long homers in the first game, and Juan Marichal went all the way and won his 24th game of the season. I watched him throughout the game, with that high leg kick and an assortment of pitches throwing guys off, and thought that he was capable of being a 30-game winner. Of course I wanted to get a shot to see what it was like against him, but I never got the call. I was watching Casey out of the corner of my eye hoping he'd call my name at some point, but he didn't.

It had only been a week or two since I first got my first glimpse of the Polo Grounds, when I first imagined Willie Mays playing in that outfield, and now I was right across from him in the visitors' dugout as his opponent. Not only was it Willie Mays, it was McCovey, Orlando Cepeda, Marichal, and even their man-ager—Alvin Dark—guys I idolized and rooted for before. Being just 20 years of age, it was a tremendous feeling to be on that same field, but it wouldn't be complete unless I played. Of course I wanted them to see me and to remember me like I had remem-bered them.

The middle game was no different—Casey never got me in. But we broke our seven-game losing streak, so that was a relief. Just before I was called up, the Mets had been shut out in their two previous games, and it happened again on my first game against Houston when we lost our 100th game. The club had gone 39 innings without scoring a single run until Joe Hicks knocked in a pair late in the game against Houston. I had never been around losing teams in any sport I ever played, and I had never seen such futility before from hitters. Some of the guys told me how often these shutouts happened, and it seemed to be bothering me more than it seemed to bother some of them.

That gnawed at me, and I wondered why Casey hadn't used me more during that short time I was there. Oh, I never would have questioned Casey Stengel and didn't talk to another player about it, but where we were going? Last place was a done deal, so it didn't seem necessary to me that the regulars were still in the lineup. I thought it was the perfect time to showcase my talents to Casey and all the other guys.

It had only been about a week since the three Alou broth-ers—Felipe, Matty, and Jesus—had played in the same outfield together for the first time in major league history (September 15, 1963). That must have been quite a sight and quite a thrill for the brothers and their families. First off, who can believe that three brothers were good enough to make the major leagues, then all be on the same team, then all be in the same outfield at the same time? I was hoping to see it for myself, but only Felipe was in the starting lineup for the final game of that series—another game with Cleon Jones sitting on the bench.

It became the Willie McCovey show in rapid order—a home run in the first, another in the second, and yet another in the fourth. On top of that, he'd already hit a pair in the opening game of the series and had 43 for the year.

I had mixed feelings at such times. Of course, I was upset McCovey was tearing up our pitching staff at will, but he was one of my home boys. So I was proud of him and simply amazed at the ease with which he made it happen, and how far those home runs traveled. I suppose I owe it to him that I got in that game, because right after his second home run, Casey looked like he'd had enough and sent me in to pinch-hit for Galen Cisco.

I flied to right but stayed in the game in left field, then got my first major league hit an inning later—a single to left off of Bobby Bolin. A few batters later I scored the first run of my career when Chico Fernandez singled me home. By then the Giants had blown the game open and led 13–2 when I got to see what I wanted to see. In the seventh inning, Alvin Dark sent Matty Alou into left, moved Felipe from right to center, and Jesus from right to left— all three brothers again in the same outfield at the same time.

When I picked up my first major league RBI on an infield groundout in the ninth, it had been quite a day with all that was going on. McCovey's three home runs, seeing all those super-stars together on one field, the Alou brothers in the same out-field together, and getting my first hit, my first run scored, and my first RBI all in that one game.

All of that was fun and exciting for me, but we had still lost the game and lost it badly. I wanted to break into the lineup and try to change what I was seeing, this culture of losing, but knew it wasn't going to change much with one man. Even if Willie McCovey had been playing for us instead of the Giants, it wouldn't have made enough of a difference. We had a long way to go, and I thought I could be a difference maker in the near future—I just needed a chance.

I only started one more game after that, and it was against the Dodgers' Sandy Koufax. He struck me out two times, but I did manage a hit off of him in between all the strikeouts. After that there was no doubt in my mind that Sandy—like Juan Marichal— was also capable of winning 30 games. I ended up with just two hits in 15 at-bats for that short stay with the Mets—not what I had wanted to do and far from what I expected to do.

Chapter 7

BUFFALO

I RODE THE BENCH for the last game of the season, the final game ever at the Polo Grounds, a loss to Philadelphia before fewer than 2,000 fans. At the end of the game, Casey said some words, and they played, "Auld Lang Syne." It was a fitting tribute to an old ballpark, and there was no one better than Casey to give it a proper good-bye. It didn't seem fitting to me that such a sparse crowd had attended that game. There were no banners or signs throughout, and the place was about as quiet as a library.

Casey was quite emotional about the whole thing, and that came as no surprise to anyone. He'd played for the Giants back in the 1920s and debuted with Brooklyn in 1912 when they were called the Dodgers (then became the Superbas again for a year, and then the Robins until changing back to the Dodgers for good in 1932). I'm sure Casey was just as emotional when Ebbets Field was knocked down in 1960.

The demise and tearing down of old ballparks certainly brought back those cherished memories that Casey had. Casey had seen some things and done some things in the game. We knew he'd been a player—he played on three World Series teams, won one with Brooklyn back in 1916, and batted close to .400 in all three. Casey had been an accomplished outfielder, and it was one of the reasons I was drawn to him. People playing the same position just seemed to gravitate more to one another because they understand better what you need to do—especially in the vast spaces of a place like the Polo Grounds.

I found it ironic that I'd been to only two ballparks other than the Polo Grounds so far and they'd been the new homes of the Dodgers and the Giants. Of course, I'd never seen Ebbets Field, but comparing the Polo Grounds to Candlestick Park was like night and day—though the way the winds blew around Candlestick was not ideal. Dodger Stadium was like a palace to me, so new and vibrant and wonderful to play in. Both cities had the kinds of fans that were really friendly to visiting players and didn't heckle you very much—especially in San Francisco.

There'd been a year's delay in the construction of the new Shea Stadium for the Mets, so that enabled me to see the Polo Grounds' last day and to understand the significance a ballpark can have on you. Of course everyone was hoping that this new stadium would represent a new beginning of good fortune for the downtrodden Mets, and I wanted to be part of that new beginning. I didn't perform like I wanted to in my short time with the club, and we'd won only 51 games. When I looked around me, the roster was full of fading veterans and a pitching staff that had six guys with 14 or more losses, and one with 22. It was a team with a poor defense, not much speed on the bases, and a number of off-season trades that seemed to have brought little in return. To my mind, going to Puerto Rico for winter ball and performing well had me believing I could make the parent club and be part of the new beginning and the new stadium. But even with a decent showing in Puerto Rico, after I went to camp with the Mets in 1964, I was optioned back to Buffalo where I stayed the entire season.

While I was concerned with my future, there'd been talk about the future of the Milwaukee Braves, and that baseball was going to relocate them to Atlanta, and the International League was put to the task of getting Atlanta ready for the Braves.

What they tried to do was to use our team as an example in getting the hotels and eating places in downtown Atlanta ready for visiting teams staying together—Black and White—in the same hotels. Our Buffalo team had a roster full of colored players like Dick Rickets, Pumpsie Green, Elio Chacon, Amado Samuel, Sammy Drake, and others. We had a lot of guys who had played in the big leagues, so we were always the lead team for everything like that.

We were in Jacksonville, and Elio Chicon went off by himself to get some dinner. Understand that we'd been warned not to go out alone, that we needed to go together and have a better chance at getting served. When Elio came back to the hotel, he told us they wouldn't serve him, and he was sobbing about it, going as far as saying he couldn't play ball anymore under such conditions. We all knew this was bound to happen and decided as a group to march back to that same restaurant to see what we could do about it.

We entered the restaurant and sat down together and waited for some service, but nobody came over to our table. We'd watched waitresses attending to other tables and just ignoring us as if we weren't even there. After a while our captain, Dick Rickets, sought out the manager to see why we weren't being served, and the manager said they weren't going to serve us. Dick reminded him that the Civil Rights Act had been signed and put into law, and we weren't leaving until we had our meal. And so we stayed put.

So they called the police, and when they arrived we told them what was going on. After a while they agreed that we were right and told the restaurant manager that by law they had to serve us. There was no confrontation or anything like that, but in the back of our minds we knew there could be. There'd been bloodshed and arrests over similar matters across the South, people being beaten up over smaller matters than this. It was a volatile time, and we had to have our guard up at all times—it's just the way things were. You couldn't get too comfortable outside of your environment, especially in an away city like Jacksonville. Anything any of us did or said could be taken as confrontational, and that usually led to violence.

We stayed at that restaurant, not just because we were hungry, but in order to make our point. We were tired of being pushed around and treated the way we'd been treated. We were tired of having to fight so many times just to get service in a restaurant. We were tired of going to the back of the bus and all that. And as I thought about all the battles that had been fought by colored folks before us, I realized this battle was part of all that, and we'd won.

Despite all that, I didn't place an order. I was worried someone in the kitchen might retaliate by doing something to the food. But I probably had nothing to worry about. With all the commotion going on around us, I hadn't noticed that most of the people that worked in the kitchen were Black, so I felt a little bit better about that, but I still didn't eat that night.

We all went back to that same restaurant the next night and sat there for at least 45 minutes, but nobody came to wait on us. It seemed like the restaurant was playing a game with us and making the point that we weren't wanted there. We weren't totally surprised but started wondering if the police had to be called in again to set things right. We were feeling somewhat frustrated and knew they wanted to demoralize us into leaving. But we weren't about to leave. We won the battle the day before and losing any ground to this sort of tactic wasn't in our plans.

So Dick sought out the manager again and told him nobody had waited on us, that we'd waited even longer for service than the day before. The manager found the waitress in charge of our table, brought her over, and she said, "I'm not gonna wait on them." He asked her why, and she said, "I don't wait on no niggers." He said, "If you can't wait on them, I'm gonna have to terminate you." She said fine and she left. We were treated nicely by another waitress and enjoyed our meal together.

Now we'd shown our resolve twice, that we weren't about to give in to any of the pressures they had placed on us. With just one more day before we had to pack our bags and go to another city, we went back to the same restaurant the next day hoping we'd be served in the usual amount of time and not be ignored like we had been for two straight days. We were sitting there for just a few minutes when the manager from the night before came out with a big smile on his face and asked us how we were doing. There was some small talk about baseball and how he appreciated our business. Then he said he had somebody who wanted to say something to us.

The waitress he'd fired the night before stood in front of us and told us she was sorry for what she'd said to us. There was sincerity in her voice, and I could tell she meant it. When she finished apologizing, we accepted it. It was good to be in that position, to be able to forgive her and to hope she would grow as a person because of what happened, because we'd grown stronger from our resolve.

We went to that place often when we were in town, and when she was working she came over with a smile and talked with us. She also started coming to some of the games and cheered for us as if we were the home team. It felt real good that a situation like that could take a new course. We'd made a friend.

And you know why? God is real. Things happen. If you can have an open mind, then you can have a change of mind. She was a decent person, but if you've been taught something all your life and suddenly, when the truth of what's right is staring you in the face—you atone from that condition you'd known your whole life. I've had teammates that way. Six months later they're different and become your best friend, really. Once they find out you don't have a tail, humanity kicks in. People aren't easily persuaded, but if you have a mindset to do what she did, to listen inside to yourself and know what you did was wrong, that's when you become a better person for it.

It was no different in baseball. The front office was always looking for a better person to sign and had started the ball rolling on our future. They'd already signed Eddie Kranepool, myself, and Ron Swoboda, then guys we didn't know yet like Buddy Harrelson, Tug McGraw, and Jerry Koosman. By then they either dealt, traded, or released veterans Roger Craig, Duke Snider, Jay Hook, Frank Thomas, Norm Sherry, and Tracy Stallard in the ever-revolving door of Mets deals. I kept my eye on all that to see what was going on with the outfielders, but Thomas was the only outfielder of the bunch that was traded, and he'd been reduced to part-time. With an outfield of George Altman, Jim Hickman, and Joe Christopher, I knew there was room for me, too.

While the Mets kept right on losing, I was fortunate to be playing for a good team, a winning team in Buffalo, where I led the team in runs scored, hits, doubles, and triples. I thought I played well enough to get another shot at the big club in 1965.

But before that, it was back to the Florida Instructional League, where we played about a 50-game schedule against mostly rookies and guys hanging on from other teams. All of us were about 20 years of age with a few exceptions. Swoboda was on our team and so was Tug. There was eight teams in the league with a good mix of good players. Boston had a team with the most notable names, guys like Mike Andrews, George Scott, Reggie Smith, Joe Foy, and Tony Horton. The White Sox had Duane Josephson and Dave Nichols. Other teams had guys like Lou Piniella, Mike

Epstein, Joe Rudi, Paul Casanova, Jim "Catfish" Hunter, Blue Moon Odom, Jim Palmer, and 18-year-old Rod Carew.

Only a handful of guys hit .300, and one of them was my future teammate Joe Foy, who hit .339. Batting .300 was always my goal, and I fell a few hits short of that, finishing at .294. But I felt I had gotten my stroke back. I didn't have even one home run, but we hit only 10 as a team, led by a guy named Willie Haas who had four home runs and led us with 24 RBIs.

Willie was our first baseman and looked to me to be a sure thing for the majors. He'd put up some big numbers with some of the Dodgers minor league teams a few years earlier, hitting over 30 home runs at Reno with close to 150 RBIs and a batting average closer to .400 than .300. That was the same team Jim Lefebvre played for, and he had similar numbers to Willie's.

Willie never made it to the majors, which was surprising. He bounced around the minor leagues for a few more years but never got the call. There were just some guys like Willie who could do it all at the top levels of minor league ball but couldn't figure it out or make the necessary adjustments needed for the majors. There were a few others in our Instructional League we thought were a sure thing—guys like and Arlo Brunsberg and Barry Shetrone—names most baseball fans would never know, but they were good players and put up some good numbers.

Brunsberg was a catcher in the Tigers system and catchers were always at a premium for any major league club. Even with Bill Freehan as their everyday catcher, Shetrone could have been used as a trading chip to another club, but that never happened for him. Arlo also bounced around the minor leagues for nearly a decade before calling it quits.

Shetrone did have some success at the major league level before coming to the Instructional League. We knew he was working hard to get back to the majors after playing parts of several seasons—mostly in the Orioles organization. That made him one of the older guys in the Instructional League, and you couldn't help but admire him for not giving up on his dream. He was with the Washington Senators organization when we saw him. He was a good hitter and batted over .300 in our league. I heard he went out to the Pacific Coast League after that and had some success, but he never got the call back up after that and was done by 1968.

You look at players like Willie Haas and Arlo Brunsberg and Barry Shetrone, and you think about how hard it is to make a major league roster and to stay on one. You know what some of the difficulties are, you think you know what the process can be, and you know there always will be another player just like you who wants to be there, too. There's an endless supply of players coming up who want to take your position away from you and hope to have long careers as major league ballplayers. You think about all that when you look around at all the talent, and you know that every one of us is thinking the same thing.

That's when you admire guys like Willie Haas and Arlo Brunsberg and Barry Shetrone. Even if you are just 20 years of age, you can see your future through those players. You know that what lies ahead of you is up to you and nobody else, and sometimes—no matter how hard you try or where you've been and what you've done before—none of that matters because today and the circumstances you are in today are what count. You take it all in—everything you see on the field, you take it all in from every player who's out there.

I took that mindset to spring training in 1965 and had a good spring. I'd worked hard in the spring, thought I'd done good enough to make the team, and was eager to find out. When the Opening Day roster was finally set, I'd reached my first goal and made the team.

But despite keeping positive thoughts in the back of my mind, by early May I was batting .156 and was sent back to Buffalo. I started thinking about some of those guys again as I made my way back to Buffalo. It was major setback to me, and I just couldn't see myself going back to Buffalo for another year, but I did.

But in the back of my mind, I thought if I did well at Buffalo, the Mets might bring me up again because of some trade or injuries or even slumps from other players. I went back to Buffalo with that in mind and got off to a great start, but after our new manager—Sheriff Robinson—saw me hit a couple of long home runs out to left field, he thought I could be turned into a power hitter.

They started to work with me on that, and I kind of got upset because that wasn't me. I knew how to turn on a pitch that was placed where I could pull it, but I had always been more of a line-drive hitter and used the whole field to my advantage—something I'd learned on the sandlots back home. I knew what to do if a pitch presented itself, but in no way was I ever purposely looking to hit a home run. And the more they worked with me on it, the more upset I became.

After a while I started pulling off the ball more and hitting ground balls to the shortstop, and I wasn't concentrating on hitting the ball where it was pitched and using the whole field. Once the opposing teams found out, they started playing me to pull instead of straight away or a bit toward right, and I lost my confidence. There were no batting instructors within the organization, so you had to rely on one or two teammates like Pumpsie Green, Choo-Choo Coleman, or Joe Christopher to help you out. Joe Christopher may not have had great success on his own, but he was a student of the game as it relates to hitting. We talked quite a bit about hitting back then, and that's when I first started to learn all the ins and outs of the process, like when to move and how to move and how to attack at the plate, your release point and all those things. Before that I was just going up there swinging and not focusing on these points. As a result it taught me a lot of things about myself, and that's when I started to become an expert myself where I could see what others were doing and knew what was needed to fix it.

I did hit 15 home runs that year, but all my numbers were down. The batting average, runs scored, RBIs, and home runs trended in the wrong direction. But I did get better throughout the year and started getting away from being the power-hitting outfielder they wanted me to be—thanks to Kerby Farrell, who replaced Robinson as manager sometime in July.

Farrell knew the kind of hitter I was and told me to go back to what I was used to doing. He knew I wasn't the power hitter Robinson had imagined I could be, and that I wasn't a pull-hitter. Once that conversation took place, I was more relaxed, and it showed in the box scores.

The Mets had to be somewhat concerned that my numbers had dropped, and it was a real concern for me as a player. But the front office had conversations with Farrell about all that, and he told them what had happened and that I'd been improving. I had the chance to prove that after our season ended and was called up again.

By that time Casey had been replaced by Wes Westrum, after Casey broke his hip during a party in July. There'd been talk that Casey would retire after that, and just a few weeks before I was called up, the Mets did announce his retirement.

When that happened, Casey was the fifth-winningest manager in major league history, and with another two years would have reached the 2,000-win mark. He had a good overall record, but managing the Mets for all those years certainly didn't tell the whole story. He'd been tied with John McGraw in winning 10 pennants and tied with Joe McCarthy with seven World Series titles. For any young Mets fan who wasn't familiar with the past, finding out something like that might have been hard to imagine.

I'd grown used to all the managers I'd already played for before, so this was nothing new for me. But Westrum didn't seem to like me much—and maybe that was because of my performance. He gave me more opportunities to play than Casey did, but I didn't make the most of them. But that didn't stop me from keeping my opinions about his managing philosophy inside, like the day in Pittsburgh when I hit my first major league home run.

We were trailing 2–0 with one out in the fifth when I came up against Bob Friend. I was looking to get on base and start some kind of rally when Westrum gave me the bunt sign. I had just come off of my first three-RBI game a few days earlier—a bases-loaded double in the first inning against the Cubs—then sat the bench for the first two games against the Pirates. I wasn't happy about that and certainly didn't want to bunt.

The team was in dead last place with more than 100 losses, and it made no sense to me that Westrum wanted me to bunt. I thought they were trying to find out as much about us as hitters, and bunting with one out and down by a run in the fifth was puzzling. On top of that the bottom of the order was behind me, with Greg Goossen and the pitcher, Tug McGraw, our scheduled batters. That made no sense, either, so I hit away and the ball landed in the left-field seats.

The only thing Westrum said to me when I got back to the dugout is if I saw him give the sign, and I said, "I saw it. I just thought better about it." He never made a big deal out of it, never fined me, and we never talked about it again.

I always was able to understand the game in situations even though I didn't talk about it or even share it with everybody else.

But when you're losing, you need to get better and you get better as a team. I knew it may have looked like I was being insubordinate—especially from a player batting just .150—but I made that split-second decision just before the next pitch from Bob Friend. I may never know if Westrum said a word about it to anyone in the front office, but he didn't bench me after that. But after that I went 1-for-15 to finish the season and ended up with an embarrassing .149 batting average.

The only solace I could take from that was all the other guys called up were hitting like I was. Guys like Kevin Collins and Buddy Harrelson, Hawk Taylor, Jimmie Schaffer, and Greg Goossen—the whole bunch of us, all below .200. But you worry about yourself and are responsible for yourself no matter what.

To say I was disappointed would be an understatement. I felt like I belonged somewhere in that outfield but had done nothing showing them I could handle major league pitching. So when the season ended, it was decided I should go back to Puerto Rico to play winter ball.

Chapter 8

PUERTO RICO

I HAD A GOOD season in Puerto Rico and finally made the Mets roster for good as the starting center fielder in 1966. I had a good rookie season, batting .275, which would have been better if I hadn't gotten hit by a pitch on the wrist by the Phillies' Bob Buhl in July. At the time I was getting close to .300, but the injury took away some of the drive and power I had before. Of course, I wasn't telling anyone about it, and I could still play, just not at 100 percent.

I was disappointed I didn't hit .300 because that was the benchmark all the great hitters used. When the season was over, only 10 players reached that .300 mark, and I felt my name could have been included with all the others—guys like Matty and Felipe Alou, Rico Carty, Richie Allen, Roberto Clemente, and others. These were elite names in baseball, and I wanted one day for mine to be among them.

I felt good that I was tied for second with 57 RBIs on the team with Ed Kranepool and second in batting average to Ron Hunt. I made the all-rookie team and finished tied for fourth for Rookie of the Year. But my buddy, Tommie Agee, won the award with the White Sox, made the All-Star team, won a Gold Glove playing center field, and finished eighth in the American League for the Most Valuable Player award. It was hard to imagine at the time that just a few years later we'd be teammates.

Tommy Helms of the Reds was our National League Rookie of the Year. I couldn't help but think if I had been on a team like he was, I might have had better stats. They had Tony Perez, Pete Rose, Vada Pinson, Deron Johnson, and Tommy Harper—guys who could really hit. I was at a disadvantage being on a Mets team without a full cast of hitters like the Reds had. There was nobody to pitch around on that club, but they could afford to pitch to me—and in no way is that a knock on my teammates or on Tommy Helms, because he was a good player and deserved the award.

The other rookies who finished ahead of me, Sonny Jackson and Tito Fuentes, as well as Randy Hundley, who tied for fourth with me, had similar lineups all around them. Sonny had Jimmy Wynn, Rusty Staub, and John Bateman. Tito had Mays and McCovey, Jim Ray Hart, and Tom Haller. Hundley had Ernie Banks, Ron Santo, and Billy Williams.

What Tommie did with the White Sox was amazing because he didn't have those types of hitters around him. They had guys like Don Buford, Jerry Adair, and Floyd Robinson—all good hitters, but none any pitcher would fear. Tommie's 22 home runs amounted to a quarter of his team's total (87), and his 86 RBIs was 34 more than the next guy in line. He was really the only power hitter on the club. I tried to imagine if Tommie had been on the Reds or the Braves or the Giants what he might have done. He was a superstar in the making. Of course, we joked about all that when we saw each other back home. But all the guys we knew from the sandlots and those earlier days were as proud as could be and had predicted things like Rookie of the Year would be in our future.

As a team we'd shown some minor improvements—losing fewer than a hundred games, for one, and not finishing last for the first time ever. But losing was still losing to me. I felt no special satisfaction in that, and because the culture of losing had been what the Mets had been known for since day one, losing didn't seem to bother some guys like it did me. I'd played for nothing but winning teams in all my sports throughout high school and after. We had a winning club in Auburn and my first year in Buffalo. But after that I was playing for losing clubs, and I wasn't happy about it.

I started to realize that losing was expected of us. It was like a contagious disease around some guys in the locker room. There was more talk about who was going to lose the game and be the one responsible for the loss than who was going to get the hit to win the game. I don't know if it was more about surviving that winning, but we just didn't exude a winning atmosphere. I think that's one of the reasons the Mets were bringing in some seasoned veterans every year—guys who were still good ballplayers but past their prime playing days—to try and show the guys what it feels like and how to go about your business from the perspective of winning programs.

I know they brought in guys like Richie Ashburn, Gil Hodges, and Duke Snider to attract some fans to the ballpark, but some guys didn't seem to be taking advantage of their presence to talk about baseball with them and learn how to improve their game. That wasn't me. I wanted to get better, and what better way could there be than to learn from all the experience of these guys? We had no hitting coaches, so I wanted to learn more about hitting. I'd never played in a long, 162-game season before and wanted to know what that was like. I wanted to know what it felt like to play on a World Series team and to actually win one.

I actually had that chance a year earlier when the Mets acquired Warren Spahn from the Braves. Spahny was quite a character, and he was a professional in every sense of the word—probably the second greatest left-hander I witnessed next to

Sandy Koufax. He'd already won more than 350 games and was still a good pitcher even at 44 years of age. I thought if he could last that long in the big leagues, so could I—as long as I stayed healthy.

Spahny was the first guy I talked to who had been in the World Series, and he shared some stories. He had a good rapport with his teammates and shared his knowledge of pitching with the others on the staff—especially the ever curious Dennis Ribant, who wanted to know everything as it related to pitching and pitching situations.

I didn't get the chance to face him when he was in Milwaukee, but I watched him intently. In my lifetime he was always one of the greats in the game and probably would have won 400 games if it hadn't been for the three years he lost during World War II. You think about guys like that at such times, guys like Spahn, Bob Feller, and Ted Williams, who all lost prime baseball years to fight for our country. I've always been mindful of that and grateful for those who served and for so many who lost their lives.

By this time I'd already gotten a world of advice from Al Jackson—advice that always stayed with me. But now I had guys like Ralph Terry and Ken Boyer to lean on—guys who'd enjoyed success and endured failure; who'd reached the pinnacle of baseball, the World Series, and suddenly found themselves on the worst team in baseball. I watched them closely to see how they dealt with all that—whether it be anger, disgust, or acceptance—and was pleased that they were professional in every sense of the word. They could have come in and gone through the motions, but they didn't, and I credit guys like Terry and Boyer for showing me all that, because I was watching.

Ralph Terry came over from Kansas City in August and didn't appear in too many games for us. It had only been four years since he'd led the American League with 23 wins and just a few years since he'd given up the winning home run to Bill Maze-roski in the 1960 World Series, then got lucky two years later on McCovey's line-drive final out of the 1962 World Series. After that'd he been dealt to Cleveland.

Ralph's locker was across from mine, and again when he came over it was just like he was there the whole time, never a stranger, but open and cordial and a great teammate. He'd tell me about all the World Series they were in, his two games against Maze-roski and McCovey, the 1961 home run race between Mantle and Maris chasing Babe Ruth, Casey Stengel, the trades, you name it. Ralph was a pleasant gentleman, and he always had a smile. He was good in the clubhouse, the kind of guy you wanted on your team—funny, pleasant, and alway willing to take the ball. It was quite something to talk to someone who was a Yankee when the Yankees were in their heyday. He even tried to get me to go golf-ing with him, but I'd never been a golfer.

Like Spahn, Ken Boyer was an icon—the very best at what he did at his position. Ken Boyer was, to me—and to a lot of folks at that time—one of the greatest third baseman to play the game. He was a great defensive player, an offensive force, and became a great teammate. He was the kind of guy who would always reach out to his teammates. He could talk about the game in a way that made you feel like you belonged in the league, that you could do it because he wasn't talking to you about what you did wrong but about how you have to be prepared to be successful. That was one of the bright spots in my early career, to have Ken Boyer as a teammate and to watch him go out on the field and perform like he did.

He told me that baseball was a business and that trades were part of the game, and to be grateful for all of it, whether playing on a World Series champion or a team in last place. We talked about not knowing why some deals were made, and I wondered how we we were able to acquire him for Charlie Smith and Al Jackson. Al was a decent pitcher, a great competitor and teammate, and he went on to have good success with the Cardinals, but we're talking about Ken Boyer. Name me a third baseman other than Brooks Robinson or Ron Santo like Boyer, because at the time those were the best in the game.

I was certain other veterans might be joining our club in the future and looked forward to learning even more from them. But being a young organization, I started to see that we were trying to add veterans and build a great farm system for all the right reasons. Sure, we were getting seasoned players at the end of their careers, but like I'd been told by Ken Boyer, baseball is a business and the club needed to draw fans to the games while waiting for the young, unknown players to develop.

People didn't realize that we were on the verge of building a great minor league system, that they were working behind the scenes to build something special. People didn't realize when they signed guys like Kranepool, myself, and a few others, then went out and got guys like Ron Hunt, that they were building toward the future. And people didn't realize that trading Hunt to the Dodgers the next season for Tommy Davis would be a huge step into making me a better hitter.

When that 1967 season rolled around, the Mets were up to a lot of wheeling and dealing again. In the off-season they released Bob Friend, Roy McMillan, and Ralph Terry, then traded Hunt and Jim Hickman to the Dodgers for Tommy Davis and traded our shortstop, Eddie Bressoud, to the Cardinals for Jerry Buchek to take Ron Hunt's place at second base.

It was quite a whirlwind of activity, but we didn't know how it all would relate to winning. And while all this shuffling was going on, what most fans didn't notice was the drafting of Duffy Dyer, Danny Frisella, Mike Jorgenson, Rod Gaspar, and Ron Cey in the amateur draft, or the signing of a young star by the name of Tom Seaver. But all those names were guys we knew little about, as were guys like Ken Boswell, Jim McAndrew, and Nolan Ryan, whom they drafted a year earlier.

Jerry Grote had become our full-time catcher a year earlier, and the departure of Bressoud left the door open for Buddy Harrelson to become our everyday shortstop. I'll never know why Houston gave up on Grote, because he was becoming the best defensive catcher in the league. He'd been there just a year, but he commanded the game, was like a bulldog, and shared my disdain for losing—only to another level. Grote hated to lose, hated the opposing players, and made no bones about it. He'd get angry if he wasn't in the lineup or being taken out for a runner.

I'd seen Buddy play shortstop when we'd been called up in December, and as the season wore on, not only was I thinking we had the best defensive catcher in baseball, now we had the best shortstop. There were a lot of good ones in the league, but defensively he was as good as anybody, and I'll say that even with today's shortstops. He had it all. He had range, a shortstop's arm, and he made all the plays. I'll put him with Grote as the best at their positions, including other guys I played with or against.

Tommy Davis had already been in two World Series, won two batting titles, been an All-Star two seasons, and in 1962 batted .346 with 230 hits and 153 RBIs. Tommy was a great baseball man. We became roommates, and that's when I really went to school on the hitting aspects of the game.

Tommy had great ideas about the art of hitting, and he showed me how he tried taking advantage of every situation, starting with the movement of the catcher before every pitch, to where the pitcher stood on the rubber. He watched every movement a pitcher made and studied tendencies to help him know what the next pitch was going to be. We talked all the time about all those things, and all of that really helped me become a better player later on.

But sometimes all the teaching and advice in the world don't deliver results right away. I started off something like 0-for-16 and was batting around .100 into May. That's a hard way to start a season, especially with great expectations building from my rookie year. I'd worked hard to reach the point where I knew I had a position and I'd be in the lineup every day. Sure enough, and even though I had a better second half, Westrum started playing Larry Stahl in center field. There wasn't much production out of Larry, either, but my average fell almost 30 points, and my production fell even more. Five home runs and 30 RBIs wasn't good enough production for an entire season.

I remember I was able to see what I was doing wrong at the plate, but I couldn't correct it no matter how many times I talked to Tommy about it. I knew I was pulling every inside pitch foul and knew that wasn't me. I was reacting to the ball too soon, and when I did hit it fair, I was still pulling out and hitting routine grounders to the shortstop. I just couldn't figure it out. We weren't studying film or anything like that then, and I started hearing boos from the fans for the first time.

New York is a hard place to play, but you can't listen to what they're saying. That's what I always told myself. When you're going good, most of them go good with you. You have two or three bad at-bats in a row, and you're a bum again. But you can't listen to all that, it can't bother you. So playing and being a good hitter is all about focus and concentration on yourself—not the people in the stands. All the sportswriters looked for a story. It doesn't have to be about your success or the team's success, they just want a story. You have to understand where you are. Like I used to tell my wife, people used to call up and ask, "Did you read the paper today?"

I would always say, "What's it about?" And they'd say it was about me. "I don't read about me," I said, "I know what I'm doing."

It didn't concern me, whatever negative thoughts people had. I just wanted to get better and contribute more to the team. A lot of things happened that taught me a lesson. I knew I was better player than I was showing after my rookie year, and I had listened to every word from Tommy Davis. Tommy hit over .300 again, and so would I.

So I went back to Puerto Rico for winter ball to try and improve on my bad season. I was frustrated with all the ups and downs I'd had so far and wanted nothing more than to be consistently good and getting into good habits again. I felt like everything Tommy had taught was sinking in and was grateful he'd spent so much time with me. I was determined to show myself, the organization, and Tommy that I was far better than what they'd seen from me that year.

We all were on one-year contracts back then, and I remember they sent my new one while I was in Puerto Rico. It was the exact same contract I had the year before, so I sent it back unsigned with a note to Johnny Murphy, now the Mets' GM. In that letter I told them I had a bad year because the coach had had a bad year. He had me in and out of the lineup, and if I'm the left fielder or the center fielder or the right fielder of the future, I needed to play so I could get better, not go in and out of the lineup for someone who's not about to help you in the future. He was a fair man, and because I stood up for myself and he understood the situation, he gave me a raise.

Vic Power was my manager in Puerto Rico. He was a talented player but had a big ego, and I actually had some problems with him. But unlike some of the other guys who also had problems with him, I didn't stay quiet about it.

We were playing a game in San Juan, and he pinch-hit for me. He had done this to other players out of spite—good players like Joe Christopher, Felix Millan, Jose Pagan, Joe Foy, and Johnny Briggs. And these were all in situations where a pinch-hitter wasn't warranted. I talked to him and asked him why he was pinch-hitting for me. I was leading the league in batting and was still hitting strong when all this happened. Pinch-hitting for me made no sense, just like when Wes Westrum gave me the bunt sign in Pittsburgh. Everybody from the other dugout was laughing when it happened, guys like Johnny Bench and Lee May were laughing at Power, not at me. They were laughing because they knew how ridiculous it was.

I was five times the player the guy he sent in for me was. I told Vic straight out, if a situation came up like that again and he pinch-hit for me, I couldn't play for him. I was there as a ballplayer making good production, and if you don't think enough of me to put in a guy inferior to my talent, then there's something wrong. He said it was his ballclub and he would run it the way he saw it.

I went to the owner of the team and said I couldn't play for Vic, that he was embarrassing everybody because of his big ego. The owner said he could see what was happening and that he'd been getting a lot of complaints from some of the other players. He asked me to be patient while he made some calls. I waited around a week and nothing was done—Power was still there—so I told them I was going home, and I left. A week or two later, they called to ask me to come back. They had fired Vic.

By then I had a reputation for being stubborn. I was a decent player and easy to get along with, but I'd always had a strong sense of what's right and what's wrong, and how I could be a conduit for righting the wrong. That's how I've been all of my life without realizing what I was doing. You know for a fact what's out there and what you're up against. *How can you make a difference when the opportunity presents itself?* is what I always asked myself. All these events had everything to do with my progress as a player and as a person, and the reputation I had as a person. I was strong-minded and didn't want a confrontation, but I never backed down from one when I knew I was right.

It was right around that time when we heard the Mets had completed a trade that sent pitcher Bill Denehy to the Washington Senators for their manager, Gil Hodges—the second time something like that had happened to Gil. The Mets had traded Gil Hodges in 1963 for Jimmy Piersall so that Gil could become the Senators' new manager. We were used to seeing players being traded for players, but to see it happen like this twice with the same person seemed unusual.

I didn't get the chance to play with Gil during the regular season when he was with the Mets, but I did play against him in an intra-squad game in spring training. I remember it was a split-squad game, and Gil was playing first base when I got a single. Just standing next to Gil was an honor for me. Here was one of the players I'd idolized as a kid and listened to his name being broadcast on our old radio during the World Series. He spoke to me, and I don't remember if I even said a word back, that's how in awe I was at the moment.

Gil set the tone for a new Mets attitude during our first team meeting in 1968. Gil told all of us that over the course of the year we'd find out we were much better than what we thought we'd be as a team, that we'd be a team to be reckoned with sooner than later. We all looked around at each other, wondering what team he was talking about.

We found out soon enough what his expectations were from each of us. We weren't just developing physically. Gil made sure he was helping develop our mindset. People don't understand about baseball that you to have the right mindset to be successful in situations because pitchers and position players remember what happened last time and how it happened. You get better by diminishing the possibility of your opponent doing better, because you remember certain situations, too.

Gil was a great baseball mind because he learned baseball in its entirety. In other words, he was a well-rounded manager. He worked well with pitchers and position players, both defensively and offensively. He was a skilled manager just like he was a skilled first baseman. Gil was good in every area of the game. Some managers were good at putting up a lineup and putting players in position, but they might not be good with pitchers or with situational moves. Gil was the kind of manager who didn't close the barn door when the horse was already gone. If he saw that you were struggling, it didn't matter who you were, we were all equals. Gil knew who was in the bullpen, he knew who was going well, he knew who the batter was, he knew what he needed at that time, lefty or righty. He didn't ask you how you were feeling, he just came and got you. Most managers had an Achilles' heal in that they didn't know when to take a pitcher out or when to keep him in. Not Gil Hodges.

There are things going on in baseball that you don't always see, but that Gil could see. He had a strategy, a plan to manage every part of the game, and that gave us confidence that we were playing for a leader of men. Even on defense we were playing all kinds of ways, even bringing me in from left field to cover third in a bunt situation. Just controlling the game and managing in ways that gave us all kinds of confidence because he knew what he was doing.

Everybody wants to win. We didn't leave spring training thinking we were the best team in baseball, we just wanted to get better and knew that we'd get better and be a team to reckon with in the future. I think that's the mindset we all had at that point. I think Gil had other plans.

Gil never blew up on the bench. He was calm, persistent, and deliberate. If a pitcher threw a certain pitch in a situation, and the guy got a hit to drive in a run, Gil wouldn't say it was the wrong pitch to throw. He'd ask them if they'd throw the same pitch in a different situation, to make them think about what they'd done wrong. He was the same way with the infielders and the outfielders. He'd confront you in such a way that he made you answer the question yourself rather than have him tell you what you might have done wrong. That's how he approached the situation. He was in complete control of everything. He was trying to teach baseball while managing the game. Gil played a pivotal role in bringing us together, because he always stressed teamwork and playing mistake-free.

Gil's philosophy and demeanor kept us focused, and we finished 1968 with fewer than 90 losses for the first time in Mets history. No longer were we the laughingstock of the league or an easy team to beat. Tom Seaver won 16 games for the second year in a row, and Jerry Koosman won 19 as a rookie. For the first time since I'd been there, we had the feeling that those guys would win every time they took the ball.

I'd been moved to left field when we traded Tommy Davis to the White Sox for Tommie Agee and Al Weis. I was sad to see Davis leave but excited that my old friend from home would join me in the Mets outfield. Tommie Agee was younger than Davis and had had a disappointing sophomore year, just like I had. A 40-point drop in his batting average, far fewer home runs than when he was Rookie of the Year, and he was ours.

Tommie's woes continued early in spring training when he was hit by a pitch from Bob Gibson. I had warned Tommie about Gibson, that he'd be knocking him down as sort of a reminder that you're not welcome here. Tommie didn't take that seriously enough, and Gibson hit him hard. After that, Tommie seemed gun-shy and had an even worse year than the year before. He looked to be headed down that road of players who were one-and-done.

While Tommie struggled, so did I—at least, at first. I barely had a .200 average by the middle of May, but it wasn't just the pitching or the cold weather that had me down, it was from a lack of sleep, and not being rested for a game.

My roommates before Tommie got there were Al Jackson and Tommy Davis. When Davis was traded, Agee became my new roommate for our away games. Tommie snored so loudly I couldn't get any sleep. It got so bad I'd throw my shoes at him to wake him up—not just a pair of shoes but several pairs. He kept snoring and I kept throwing, and soon enough I was all out of shoes. Even when went out to eat together, I'd slip back to the hotel before him in order to get some sleep before he got back, but that trick never worked.

Right at the end of spring training, there must have been a writer next door to our room, and he brought in some kind of recording of somebody snoring really loudly, and turned it up all the way so everyone could here it. I guess the word got out, because Gil gave both of us private rooms after that.

Chapter 9

TURNING POINT: HOUSTON (1969)

EVERY TEAM WANTS to get off to a good start and win its opener, especially our team. We'd lost every Opening Day since I'd been there, and the Mets franchise as a whole had never won an opener in their first seven years. It was important for us to start the season with a win and break that pattern—to start off with a win, be 1–0 and at least tied for first place, if only for a day.

Everything seemed to be in our favor. Tom Seaver was our starting pitcher, we were playing at home, and our opponent was the expansion Montreal Expos. Yes, we'd lost all of our Opening Day games, and odds were pretty good that this new team would too. But that's not how baseball works.

They had a decent lineup—hitters like Rusty Staub, Mack Jones, and Maury Wills—but it wasn't a strong lineup top to bottom. In the very first inning, however, Bob Bailey doubled home two runs, and we fell behind 2–0. But Tommie Agee cleared the bases in the bottom of the second with a three-run double, and we were feeling pretty good with a 3–2 lead and Seaver on the mound. From that point on they kept coming and took a 4–3 lead on a home run by Dan McGinn in the fourth. But we rallied again with run-scoring singles by Rod Gaspar, Ken Boswell, and myself, and led 6–4 after four.

It was rare that we scored six runs in any game, and this was just the fourth inning. A year earlier we had a great record (13–4) when we scored six runs or more, and we knew it was just a matter of time before Seaver settled down, because he always did. But he had struggled, and Gil pulled him after five. There was no stopping Montreal over the final four innings. Coco Laboy and Rusty Staub homered, and we trailed 11–6 going into our half of the ninth.

When Duffy Dyer hit a pinch-hit homer to make it 11–10, who knew it was a sign of things to come? Who knew that moments like that would become part of a season where contributions came from everyone? From the role players to the starters and on down the line, home runs like Duffy Dyer's would become the norm later in the year. But we still lost the game 11–10, stranding the tying run at second and the winning run on first.

That game was certainly an anomaly to our season. We were supposed to have one of the best pitching staffs, if not *the* best pitching staff in the league, and we'd given up 11 runs. Our offense was supposed to be one that struggled for runs, but we'd scored 10. We couldn't afford to lose games in that manner, and from that game forward, we seldom did. Turns out the combined run total for that game was the highest of any game on our schedule that year.

After a 2–2 start, we fell below .500 for a while and were just 12–15 when we hosted Houston for a three-game series in May at Shea Stadium, bringing back memories of the crazy games we played against the Astros a year earlier, starting with a record-breaking, 25-inning, 1–0 loss in April at the Astrodome.

That marathon of a game ended on an error by Al Weis, an easy grounder that looked like a sure double play that might have hit the cutout of the Astroturf and went under his legs. Whatever it was, that game took over six hours to complete, and at the time it was the longest scoreless game and the longest night game in major league baseball history.

I'd gone in to pinch-run for Art Shamsky in the ninth inning and ended up with six at-bats. I went 1-for-6, but that was nothing compared to what Agee and Swoboda did that day. Taking an 0-for-4 or 0-for-5 collar is one thing, but they both went 0-for-10. Being that it is was only our fifth game of the season, I think their batting averages dropped about 150 points each from just that one game.

In August that same year we got into a nasty brawl with the Astros in the Astrodome. Maybe the Astros didn't like the fact that we were ahead of them in the standings at the time, I don't know, but they always seemed like a menace to our organization. I wasn't there for the start of the rivalry when the Mets and Astros came into the league together in 1962, but during my first full season in 1966, I heard some of the veterans talk about the rivalry and how poorly the Mets had done against Houston. The Mets didn't have a good record against any team back then, but to go 8–26 their first two seasons against another expansion team, split 18 games in 1964, and go 4–14 in 1965 was cause for concern and probably was embarrassing to the organization.

It was 1966 when that trend started to turn around. Or at least we thought it did—because it didn't last very long. We beat them 11 out of 18 times and managed to crawl out of the National League cellar for the first time in our history. It doesn't sound like much, but a good season for a Mets fan at the time would be a year we didn't finish in last place, a year with fewer than 100 losses, and a year where we finished ahead of Houston. Two out of three that year gave us some hope for the future.

We fell back to our old ways against Houston in 1967. Because of our 7–11 record against them, they finished eight games ahead of us, and again we were in last place with more than 100 losses. I'm sure it was frustrating to the Mets fans who'd been around since the beginning, to see the other expansion team always just a little bit better than us. The Astros had some pretty good arms back then—guys like Mike Cuellar, Dave Giusti, Larry Dierker, and Don Wilson were real pros. And they had some good offensive players, like Jimmy "the Toy Cannon" Wynn, and an up-and-coming Joe Morgan.

That rivalry seemed to take a new turn just before the brawl of '68 broke out, when the Astros' Doug Rader slid into third after hitting a triple and came up from his slide with an elbow to the face of our third baseman, Kevin Collins. We knew it was bad for Kevin, and we reacted to it right away.

Pitcher Don Cardwell decked Rader, and Tommie Agee bolted in from center field and took out two more guys. I certainly wasn't going to stand around and do nothing—I was all of that when it came to protecting a teammate. I was a teammate, and if you harmed my teammate you harmed me. And if my teammate was in a situation, it was my situation, too. I punched out John Bateman, and everybody was hitting and running and jumping on each other, even some of the coaches. By the time the thing was over, Kevin was being treated for a broken jaw, had to be taken out on a stretcher, and tempers continued to flare. It took a while to calm that down.

But 1969 was a new season, and the Houston Astros weren't on our minds—at least, at first. That 1969 season was certainly a miracle season in every sense of the word for the Mets. It's hard to explain with all that had happened that season, especially with so many close games we played and all the come-from-behind wins. When you look at all the timely hitting and the great pitching and defense we had, it's almost hard to believe how we fared against the Houston Astros. Don't get me wrong, they were a good team, and just like us, they reached the .500 mark for the first time in their history that season.

Along with Wynn and Morgan, they had a good hitting team with players like Curt Blefary and Denis Menke. And Dierker and the flame-throwing Wilson were tough, but neither was feared like Bob Gibson or Sandy Koufax. They were beatable pitchers, and our staff was solid from top to bottom. We should have matched up better against them. They were an average team but played us like they owned us. I don't know if they kept that brawl in the backs of their minds to motivate them when they played us, but it sure didn't work both ways. If anything, we should have been more motivated than they were, because they were the ones who started the fight.

It's hard to explain how one team can do what they do against another team in a given season, but the Astros went 10–2 against us in 1969 and did even better against Montreal, winning 11 of 12 games. The Astros had winning streaks of 10 and eight games that year, and both our club and the Expos were right in the middle of those streaks because the Astros' schedule had us and the Expos playing them in back-to-back series all season. Twelve of those 18 wins from those two winning streaks were against our two teams.

We'd made it back to .500 by winning the first three games of a seven-game road trip in mid-May, then lost a blowout game to the Braves, pushing us back under at 18–19. We still felt pretty good going into Houston, but the Astros were playing good ball. They'd just swept Montreal and had a five-game winning streak. Sometimes you're the hot team, and other times it's them. This time it was them. They stayed hot and swept us in three games that weren't close, then went on to sweep Philadelphia for a 10-game winning streak that finally ended the same day we began our 11-game winning streak.

Of course, I didn't know what we were about to do at the time, but knowing the Astros were the hottest team in baseball told me that things were coming around for them and we were close behind. But our concentration wasn't on the Astros, the first-place Cubs, or any other team. It was on us.

Only a quarter of the season had been played, and though we showed no progress in the standings, and despite getting swept by Houston, we knew we were a better team than that. The feeling at the time was that we weren't a great ballclub but that we were getting better each day. We finished near the bottom the year before, and when we looked around the league we saw some good clubs like Chicago, St. Louis, Pittsburgh, Los Angeles, San Francisco, Atlanta, and now even Houston.

When you look at pitchers like Tom Seaver, Jerry Koosman, Tug McGraw, Nolan Ryan, and on and on, you've got to feel like you're better. And with Agee playing great in center field and Swoboda, Shamsky, Kranepool, Harrelson, and Grote, we looked like a real professional team for the first time since I'd been there. I saw a competitive professional ballclub that could beat any team on any given day. True, we were under .500 at the time, and even though we felt we were getting better, I always felt like any day somebody was going to wake up and contribute more. The Gil Hodges speech in spring training, when he told us we were a lot better than what we thought we were and it would be proven throughout the season, was what I remembered as we started the next homestand against the other expansion team—the San Diego Padres.

One thing you never do in baseball is take another team for granted. It was our first look at the Padres, and they'd done what most expansion teams had done before—lose games by wide margins. A few weeks earlier they'd lost to the Cubs 19–0, a week before that 12–0 to the Reds, and 14–0 to the Dodgers earlier in the season. They'd lost eight of nine coming into Shea, so the

Padres reminded me a lot of us when I first came up. Everybody knew they'd have their struggles, but we felt pretty good about starting the homestead with two games against them before taking on the Giants and the Dodgers.

Then we lost the first game to the Padres, another disappointing one-run loss where we had plenty of chances but couldn't get it done for Jim McAndrew. I went 2-for-5 but made the last out of the game—a groundout to second base. We'd dropped five in a row and stayed firmly in fourth place, nine games behind the Cubs with an 18–23 record, and not thinking at all about first place. Just to get back to .500, we would have to win six of our remaining seven games on the homestand before facing our longest road trip of the year starting on the West Coast against the Padres, Dodgers, and Giants, then ending up in Philadelphia before coming back home again.

But one thing I never did was dwell on those kinds of mind games, because one thing about a baseball season is there's always another game tomorrow. We had to put that game behind us and move on to the next, and that was reinforced all season long by Gil Hodges. He wouldn't allow us to have a letdown. He was steady, coaching and managing the ballgame in its entirety.

Our first win of that 11-game winning streak was the turning point and defined our season with all the close, hard-fought wins we had. It seemed like we were always in one-run games, but just like Mets teams from the past, we'd lost most of them and had lost our fair share already for the season. We'd had plenty of chances to score earlier in that game against the Padres, but we left a few men on base a couple of times and couldn't manage a hit when we needed it. Koosman was his usual self. He went 10 innings and then Tug came on in the 11th. He walked a couple of batters but was bailed out by a double play and struck out their big power hitter, Nate Colbert, to end the inning.

I reached on an error to begin the bottom of the 11th, and after one out Swoboda singled. Then Grote was walked intentionally to load the bases. It was a good strategy by the Padres. Buddy Harrelson was up next and then Tug after him. Buddy was having a decent season to that point, but he didn't hit for power. Even his fly balls to the outfield usually weren't hit far enough to score the runner from third, and any ground ball to the infield could result in two. With Tug on deck, we'd probably pinch-hit for him if Buddy made an out. But Buddy came through this time. He singled to left center, and I trotted home for the only run of the game.

The rest of that homestead was pretty much the same script, only a new hero every night. The following night we trailed the Giants 3–0 into the seventh inning. McCovey had homered off of Seaver, and we couldn't get anything going off a tough lefty in Mike McCormick.

At the time we weren't known for coming from behind to win games. Our good pitching and defense kept us in most games—having the lead and keeping it led to most of our wins. That all started to change when Ron Swoboda homered in the seventh and singled in another run in the eighth to go along with Rod Gaspar's homer earlier in the inning. After Agee singled, Frank Linzy came in to face me, and I kept the inning alive with another single before Joe Gibbon replaced Linzy. Then Duffy Dyer came in as a pinch-hitter—a stressful situation for any player—and he felt it at that moment. He'd only batted a handful of times all season, but his pinch-hit, three-run homer against Montreal on Opening Day was fresh in people's minds, and the big crowd was hoping he'd do it again.

I don't know what Gil said to Duffy when he went up to the plate, but Gil always told each of us to be ready at all times because you never knew when it would be your time. That mindset was stressed all the time to us, so I knew Duffy was ready to go. And as I got my lead from third, Duffy singled me home to put us ahead. There were over 50,000 fans in the ballpark, and it was as loud as I could ever remember when I crossed home plate. When Ron Taylor struck out Willie Mays, Willie McCovey, and Bobby Bonds in the ninth, you could tell something special was happening.

After eight more wins on the homestand, our 18–23 record had turned into 28–23, and we'd moved up two notches into second place, unfamiliar ground for the team and our fans. Though we were now in second place, we'd only picked up 1½ games on the red-hot Cubs. But we weren't thinking about first place just yet. We certainly had enjoyed our winning streak, but with more than 100 games left, our concentration was on ourselves and doing better each and every night.

We picked up more ground over the next several weeks and stayed in second place, five games out of first. After a 4–3 road trip against the Cubs and Expos, we returned home for 10 games at the end of July, including three against the pesky Astros.

We knew they had our number to that point in the season. Up and down their lineup it seemed that everybody on their team had good swings, hit the ball hard, had good at-bats against our great pitching staff. They just seemed to wear out our pitching. I never could figure it out, because it didn't just happen in Houston, it happened at Shea.

They were putting a good whupping on us, winning the first game of the doubleheader 16–3, including an 11-run ninth inning. I remember sitting in the dugout at the end of that inning, and our team looked like we were enjoying it. I'm sure Gil Hodges noticed that and kept it inside as we prepared for the second game of the doubleheader.

Of course, we weren't expecting them to do it again, but they weren't through with us yet, scoring another 10 runs in the third inning. It was during that inning when our season changed for us. Left-handed hitter Johnny Edwards came up to bat for Houston, and even though we played him a bit to left, he hit the ball down the line, and I knew I couldn't stop him from going to second because the field was a muddy swamp, and I had a bad ankle. But I wanted to stay in the lineup because I was swinging the bat well.

We'd had a conversation about me staying in the lineup before the game, and I told him as long as I wasn't hurting the ballclub defensively, I wanted to stay in the lineup. I was in such a zone at the time. I didn't want to come out of the lineup and risk losing the groove I was in. The bad ankle wasn't going to heal overnight, and I was pretty sure it wasn't going to get any worse because we were taping it up before every game. It was an old football injury that started coming back to me. But we were getting our asses kicked, and we seemed to be accepting that in a way that wasn't pleasing to Gil Hodges.

After Edwards's double, Gil came out of the dugout, and naturally I thought he was taking Nolan out of the game. When he passed the pitcher's mound, I thought he was going to have some conversation with Buddy. But when he passed Buddy, I looked behind me at the bullpen and didn't see anything happening there. Suddenly he was in front of me and said, "What's the problem, ankle bothering you?"

"No. It's no worse than what it's been," I said.

"Well," he said, "do you think you could have held him to a single?"

"Held who to a single?" I said.

"The batter...Edwards."

"No, no way I could have held him. The ball was hit right down the line." Maybe Gil was thinking more about the way we reacted to losing the first game of that doubleheader, I don't know. Johnny Edwards had already had a single earlier in the inning, and his double blew the game open at that point. I thought about all that when I said to Gil, "Look down at what we're standing in."

He looked down, and my feet and his feet were under water. I said again there was no way I could get to that ball any quicker than I did, and he said, "You're right. You know what, you've got a bad ankle, anyway, and you shouldn't even be out here. I think you ought to come out of the ballgame."

"Fine," I said. "You're the manager."

That's when we walked back to the dugout together.

When I was walking back to the dugout, I didn't have any feelings about that one way or another because we'd had a conversation about it and were getting our tails kicked. I sat down for a while in the dugout, but when I went back to the locker room, that's when the fanfare hit with the writers asking questions.

I didn't think for one second Gil was trying to embarrass me, but that's what they were asking. I thought he was trying to make a statement, not to me, but to the team. I think I was leading the league in batting at that point, and *we* were getting our asses kicked, not because Cleon Jones was loafing on one play. I thought he was trying to make a statement to the ballclub that we needed to wake up, and if he could talk to me by coming out and dealing with me that way, then everybody else would wake up and play better.

But the Astros just continued to hit line drive after line drive, it wasn't like we were making any errors—they were just driving the ball and drawing walks, stealing bases, and everything else. Even their pitcher, Larry Dierker hit a home run after I was taken out of the game. I thought it was unusual that all the hitters in their lineup were having such good at-bats against the pitching staff they were facing. They pounded Gary Gentry that inning, and they'd pounded Cal Koonce and Ron Taylor in the first game. It's not very often you see a team scoring double digits in an inning, and they'd scored 21 runs over the last four innings. I'm sure all of that played on Gil Hodges's mind when he came out to get me.

When I went into the clubhouse, everybody said I was upset—this, that, and the other thing. But nothing happened. To me, the writers were just trying to get me to say something to stir things up. I hadn't even thought about it and didn't feel it was an embarrassing situation for me because I wasn't embarrassed. I knew Gil Hodges, and I knew what kind of a person he was. No way would he try to embarrass me or anybody else. He was trying to make a statement, and it worked, because after that everybody was on the balls of their feet playing the game of baseball and doing it well. In my opinion, right after that was when we started becoming a team.

It became a topic of conversation, and some people added their own opinion of what had taken place. It was a wake-up call to me. That one play didn't define who I was or what I was doing. It was an ingenious move, as I see it today, for Gil Hodges to come out and make a statement like that, because it resonated with the whole team. Gil saw that we were sitting back, getting our tails kicked, and seemed to be okay with it. That not the ballclub he represented and managed or talked about in spring training.

I knew he saw that none of us seemed to be making any adjustments and nobody was cheering from the bench—no chatter or anything showing we were mad or embarrassed at what was happening. I don't think anybody on the ballclub thought that I was loafing or could have held Edwards to a single. That was one incident in one game. The ball hit down the left-field line, and I ran as hard as I could in the conditions I was under. By the time I got to that ball, he was already coasting into second.

You can run film on me from now to Christmas, and you won't ever see any differences in my approach. But the field conditions were so bad at the time, it may have looked like I was loafing, even though I wasn't. It was so wet, the ball stopped rolling— that shows you what the conditions were like. I know it was a wake-up call because I heard the chatter in the clubhouse, that if Gil would do that to me, they knew he could do it to them.

I had no negative thoughts about Gil Hodges or what happened. Gil said right after that he thought I should rest my ankle for a couple of games. He called me into his office and asked me when I thought I'd be be ready to go, and I just said I'd let him know. I couldn't run the way I normally could, but I was swinging the bat well at the time and wanted to be out there. My wife said to me repeatedly, "You should never have been out there in the first place." But I'm a ballplayer and a team player, and as long as I was contributing to the team, I was satisfied.

We woke up mentally after that incident but started losing more ground to the Cubs. They'd lost to the Giants the same day Houston blew us out, and we were just 5½ games out of first place. Then they won their next seven games, including a three-game sweep against the Astros in Houston. We went into Houston a few days later, thinking it was time to even the score, but they did it to us again. They swept us three straight, and just like that we were 10 games behind the Cubs and in third place. But what happened with me out in left field woke up the team. Our best was yet to be.

Chapter 10

MAKING OUR MOVE

ABOUT THREE WEEKS before getting swept by the Astros, we split a doubleheader with the Expos just before the All-Star break that kept us five games behind the Cubs. I was batting .341 and trailed the Pirates' Matty Alou by just 13 points when I was elected to my one and only All-Star team as a starter. It was a dream come true being on that All-Star team because the league was full of so many great players—and especially nice that Seaver and Koosman would share the moment with me as teammates.

But the National League outfield was packed with stars. Pete Rose didn't make that team, and yet he won the batting title that year. Pete, Billy Williams, Lou Brock, Willie Stargell—when I looked around the league at guys who didn't make it, and suddenly I was one who did, it was very surreal and humbling. You've got Willie Mays and Hank Aaron as perennials on the team, and even Willie wasn't in the starting lineup that year.

They talk about the 1971 All-Star team and all the future Hall of Famers, but we had our share with 13 on the National League alone and six from the American League. And because it rained the night the game was scheduled, I had more time to get to know some of them. The locker room was hilarious. You had to pinch yourself being part of that group.

When you've got Ernie Banks in the clubhouse, there wasn't a moment of rest. "Let's play two." "What about them Cubs?"

"What about that Fergie Jenkins?" "What about that Billy Williams?" He'd go on about the whole team. "Oh, that Santo, he's the best third baseman in baseball. Kessinger…he's an All-Star." Banks just went on and on, and on even in the dugout he never stopped, constantly bugging our manager, Red Schoendienst: "Put me in there, Red. Let me get in, Red. Let me get in, Red." He never stopped. He even started on me and the Mets. "You just lucky," he'd say. "No way the Mets gonna pass us in the standings. No way any team will, we the team to beat, you'll see."

And it wasn't just at the All-Star Game, he was like that every time you'd get on first base. You'd get a good hard hit off of one of their pitchers, and he'd say, "Ahhh, you just lucky. That Fergie, he's a great pitcher. How did you get that hit? I'll tell you how you got that hit…you're lucky, that's all. A hit off of Ferguson? Nothing but luck." Then you'd come back to the bag after the next pitch, and he'd still be talking about it: "You hit a nothing pitch." And I'd say, "How can a great pitcher throw a nothing pitch?" And he'd say, "You was lucky." Banks was a promoter of baseball. He should have been the face of baseball, because he was always promoting the game wherever he was.

Of course, we were eager to get out of the gates from the All-Star Game and onto a winning streak, but after getting swept by the Astros, we'd gone 9–12, lost five games in the standings, and trailed Chicago by 10 games with a third of the season left. It was no time to be panicking, but we'd fallen into third place behind the surging Cardinals. They'd been 16 games behind and seven games under .500 by early July, but they'd gone 26–7 to pass us in the standings, shaving seven games off the Cubs' lead. We'd been nine games ahead of St. Louis when they made their move, and since the Cubs and Mets had played .500 ball during that same time, the Cardinals had become a contender. Perhaps Ernie Banks had been right about us.

But we had to concentrate on ourselves and on what we knew we were capable of doing. We came back to New York for a crucial 10-game homestand against the same teams we'd won seven of eight from during that 11-game winning streak. We all knew the importance of winning, and winning now. That 11-game streak certainly created interest and a spark—we felt good being the second-place team in our division and looking up. We thought we already had a good year because we were in second place that late in the season, and the icing on the cake was in front of us.

But we'd dropped to third, and with every game the season grew shorter. Playing .500 ball wasn't going to get it done. We were a young team that had left spring training without an inkling of how good we were. We didn't start the season thinking we were the best team in baseball, we just wanted to get better, knowing that we'd be a team to reckon with in the future. And even though we'd lost ground in the standings since that 11-game winning streak, I think that was the mindset we all had at that point. But I think Gil Hodges had other plans.

Because of rainouts and the schedule, we had to play back-to-back doubleheaders over two days against the Padres—a difficult task for any team's pitching staff. Usually doubleheaders ended up being split, but we'd already played 13 doubleheaders to that point, winning 16 of the 26 games with five sweeps, including consecutive sweeps over St. Louis and Philadelphia in June. By the time the season was over, we'd played 22 doubleheaders, sweeping half of them and going 30–14 in those 44 games. And because we had so many rainouts earlier, we played 11 doubleheaders during August and September—the months when pitchers start getting tired and breaking down some. With the Cubs playing just three in the last two months of the season, the advantage certainly seemed to be in their favor.

People ask me all the time how we did what we did that season, and I always point out our great defense, clutch-hitting, and great pitching—especially guys who could get us a win after a loss. Seaver won nine of his games after a loss. Koosman won six, and even Tug McGraw did the same. Gentry did it five times. You go on down the line, and you could see the contributions from our pitchers all season long. With so much attention by the press given to Seaver and Koosman, Ron Taylor led the club with 13 saves that year and also notched nine victories.

But our record in doubleheaders has to be part of the equation. And it wasn't only our record in those games, but the way those wins featured different players doing different things to win. Tug pitched a complete-game win over the Cubs early in the season. Cal Koonce pitched four innings in relief in several of those games. Jack DiLauro got his only win of the season against the Expos. Koosman and Cardwell knocked in the only runs of the games in consecutive 1–0 wins against the Pirates.

When you play so many doubleheaders in one season, there has to be depth on your bench with plenty of playing time to go around. That's what made it fun for guys because they knew they'd likely be starting one of those games—especially in the catching position. Grote couldn't catch both ends most times, so we needed J.C. Martin and Duffy Dyer to contribute.

J.C. did most of his damage in those 30 wins. He batted well over .400 with seven RBIs and a home run. Duffy hit a game-winning homer in another game, and Grote batted around .280 with another seven RBIs. From the catching position alone in those 30 wins, that trio batted close to .320.

There's way to know why some of our performances stood out in those 30 wins, but some of the batting averages from some of the guys in those 30 wins helps explain why we were so successful in 1969. Ken Boswell and I batted over .400; and Shamsky and

Agee were right behind. Even Al Weis—whom everybody called a "light-hitting shortstop"—seemed to excel in those games. Not only did Al bat over .300 in the 16 games he started, he knocked in 10 runs—nearly half of his season total. As for me, my big moment came late in April against the Cubs.

We'd just lost the first game to them after taking a 6–4 lead into the ninth. Two errors and a Randy Hundley home run turned a sure win into a loss, and we weren't feeling too good about the way it all happened. To make matters worse, I struck out looking to end the game. I might add it was the only game all season long that Tom Seaver pitched in relief, striking out the opposing pitcher, Phil Regan, for the final out for the Cubs.

We went into the ninth inning of the second game in a scoreless tie. We'd managed just three hits to that point against Rich Nye, but when Rod Gaspar opened the inning by reaching on an error and Ken Boswell walked, I knew I had a good chance to come to the plate and knock in the winning run with just a single somewhere. Then when Ed Charles flied out to third, I came to bat.

My wife and I had something planned for after the game, so the last thing I wanted was for the game to go into extra innings. I remember saying in the dugout that my wife and I had plans, and we don't get paid for overtime, so I didn't want to do any. I normally don't think about hitting a home run, but that's what I was thinking at the time. I got lucky and got a pitch I could hit off of Rich Nye for a walk-off homer and a split that we should have swept.

But the schedule down the stretch certainly favored the Cubs. Needing to play only three doubleheaders versus our 11 in August and September—that's a big advantage for any team, especially a Cubs team that seemed to be overusing some of their pitchers. I find it interesting that we finished eight games ahead of the Cubs in the standings, and when the season ended, the Cubs' record in doubleheaders was just 14–16—a nine-game difference from ours. But If any series could define our season, if any four games over two days could show what we were made of, it was that series against the Padres.

We scored just 10 runs in the four games against them, yet won all four games. And like they'd done all season, our pitchers came through for us again. Seaver pitcher a four-hit, 2–0 shutout; McAndrew won 2–1; Koosman pitched a gutsy, complete-game, 3–2 win; and Cardwell pitched seven innings in the series' final game for another 3–2 win.

Certainly our offense didn't stand out, as we managed only 14 hits in the final three games and 23 for the series—games most teams would have normally lost. But the clutch hitting and contributions from so many guys in all four games were equally responsible for the sweep and prove what I've said all along— that 27 guys contributed to what happened in 1969.

Agee broke a scoreless game with a single in Game 1; I hit a home run in the second game to tie it in the fourth, and Grote won it with a pinch-hit single late in the game. In the third game, Duffy Dyer—as he had on Opening Day against the Expos— clubbed a three-run homer in the seventh to erase a 2–0 Padres lead; and in the final game of the series, Bud Harrelson knocked in two runs with a bases-loaded triple late in the game and scored on J.C. Martin's pinch-hit sacrifice fly to win it.

It was a rare thing to see such contributions from so many players in consecutive games that resulted in four wins, but not in our season. After that series was over, we jumped back into second place and never fell back. The next game against the Giants was a classic pitchers' duel and another incredible 1–0 win that took 14 innings to decide—a game in which Giants ace righty Juan Marichal went the distance, giving up the game-winning home run to Agee in the 14th.

For the nearly 50,000 in attendance, it was yet another sign in our miracle season that we were still in it. We'd won five of the most hard-fought games in a row and cut the Cubs' lead down to seven games. After going 6–1 the next week, with the Cubs going 2–6 and the Cardinals 2–5, we bolted past the Cardinals by 5½ games into second place, cut the Cubs' once-commanding lead down to 2½. More importantly, we had the same number of losses as they had. All we had to do was take care of business. But the next week we lost some ground, losing four of seven games with the Cubs winning five of six, putting them three games ahead of us in the loss column.

They always tell you not to look too far ahead in the schedule and to take the games one at a time, but the Cubs were coming into Shea in just a few days after we opened a four-game set with Philadelphia. Everybody was looking ahead to that series. The press was doing it; the fans were doing it; and as hard as it was to not think about it, all of us were thinking about it. But we knew what mind games can do to a player, and that if we let our guard down we could fall even further behind. But when we won three of four from the Phillies and the Cubs got swept at home by the Pirates, the Cubs' lead stood at just 2½ games.

Since August, when we were nine games out, we had improved by leaps and bounds. So we were confident each and every night that we were going to win the ballgame. You don't know if you can make up nine or 10 games because it doesn't matter how well you do, you still need the other team to falter some. So you couldn't say in July or even August that we were going to catch them, because we had to continue to play great baseball down the stretch.

I don't think we really understood until late August, when the Cubs came in for those two games, that we were better than them. We thought we were better than everybody because we were beating everybody, and we thought now we were the team to beat even though we were still a few games behind. In late August we saw that they couldn't get anybody out of the bullpen to stop rallies—something we hadn't seen in July or early August. And we knew if we continued to play well—and Gil Hodges made sure of that—we thought we could catch them.

We were feeling good, and I think we knew at that point that something great was about to happen. Nobody was saying it, we just went out and played baseball, trying not to make mistakes, taking one game at a time, and using every player on the roster all the way down to the last man.

And that was the difference between Gil and the Cubs' manager, Leo Durocher. Gil got the most out of everybody, and I can't say it enough. Every player was involved and every player contributed. If you go back to Gene Mauch and the 1964 Phillies, they just needed one or two games to clinch with more than a week to play. But Mauch only pitched two guys down the stretch run—Jim Bunning and Chris Short—and look what happened there. Winning is not a one-man show, it's a team effort. When you have team participation, the motivation is different, and that's when you win. When Leo decided to use the same guys every day, they got worn out—especially under the hot sun at Wrigley in the dog days of summer.

I will say this. I've never been tired in a baseball game in my life. Your adrenaline doesn't allow that. I remember wearing myself out in a pregame once, and after that I changed my ways. I knew who I was. I knew my limits. I knew when I needed extra batting practice and I knew when I didn't need any batting practice. There's a saying—"Know thyself"—and it's good advice. The season is 162 games plus playoffs and the World Series, but that's what you get in shape for. As I think about it, I go back to even my high school days when I played football. When the whistle blew to start the game, I played offense, defense, and special teams. I stayed on the field the whole game until it was over. That's the mindset I had about sports in general. You don't get tired of playing what you love to do.

What you can't allow is for yourself to get mentally tired. You prepare yourself to make it fun, to remember it's a game that you love and get paid to do. How many people can say that? Baseball to me was meant to be played in the daytime. I never had any problems with daytime or sunlight or heat, but when you're playing the same people each and every day, it's bound to take its toll. I keep referencing this, but we had a roster of 27 players, and every one of them took part. Every one had a role in what took place. But when you play the same eight guys each and every day—especially when most of them were over 30—it makes a difference with all those day games at home.

But Leo never learned that. They didn't have a great bench or great relievers. Phil Regan pitched almost every day, and by August he was having trouble getting people out. During that stretch run of the final two months, when the Cubs needed him most, his ERA was almost six runs a game, and some games he didn't get even one batter out.

That's when we felt like we were in control of everything—we were up-and-coming and getting better with each and every game. Gil Hodges wouldn't allow us to beat ourselves, so that made it more difficult for other teams to beat us. We weren't making errors or throwing to the wrong base or missing the cut-off man, and we weren't running ourselves out of big innings. We were playing major league baseball the way it should be played.

Chapter 11

THE BLACK CAT

WE'D PULLED TO within 2½ games of the Cubs and had them at home for an important two-game series. With Koosman and Seaver lined up to face Bill Hands and Fergie Jenkins, we had who we wanted against their best. Koosman had won four of his last five decisions, and Seaver had won his last five, so we were pretty confident we could take them.

Shamsky started in left that game, and it was tough for me to sit out because of the magnitude of the situation. Every ballplayer wants to take part in a crucial series like that one and not watch it from the bench, but when Agee took Bill Hands deep for a two-run homer in the third, I was cheering just as loud and hard as the 43,000 fans in attendance.

Our 2–0 lead lasted until the sixth, when three straight singles by Don Kessinger, Glenn Beckert, and Billy Williams, plus a Ron Santo sacrifice fly, tied the game at 2–2. The tie lasted an inning as Agee started a rally with a leadoff double to center and came home on a single by Wayne Garrett for the final run of the game. Koosman capped it off by striking out the final two batters of the game. We'd pulled to within 1½ games of the Cubs, but more importantly were even with them in the loss column. With Seaver going up against Fergie the next night, we felt that the tide had finally turned.

It had been exactly two months since Seaver had his perfect game spoiled by Cubs backup outfielder Jimmy Qualls with one out in the ninth at Shea. With a a lineup full of guys like Banks, Santo, and Williams, the last guy you'd think would break it up was someone like Qualls. But because they often don't know much about them, great pitchers sometimes have problems with players like that. What can you say? He got a pitch to hit and he hit it.

Just before Qualls came to bat, Randy Hundley tried beating out a bunt, but Seaver fielded it cleanly and threw him out at first. We all understood the importance of starting a rally, but for a player to bunt for a hit in a situation like that was really against the unwritten rules of baseball. I'm sure if Randy had beaten it out for a hit, there would have been some hot tempers from both sides that would have been long-lasting—especially if it had been the only hit. But Randy didn't have to worry about that as we concentrated on Jimmy Qualls and where to set up on defense for him.

During those situations, you're very much aware of what's happening on the field, so on defense you're trying to play where you can keep the guy from getting a hit. I cheated a couple steps forward to try and take something away. Sure, it could go over my head for a hit, but most hits wind up in front of you. You think about that in the field. It just happened that he got good wood on it, and that was that. I knew the second he hit it there was no way Tommie or I could reach it, and it fell in between us. Tommie got to the ball and tossed it back to the infield, and we didn't really say anything to each other. A couple shakes of the head and disappointment on our faces was all that seemed right.

I watched Seaver sort of drop his shoulders and his head, probably wishing he could get that pitch back. He got the ball back and swiped the rubber a few times, and that's when the crowd of almost 60,000 made the most noise I'd ever heard at any game before.

The sound was deafening, and I swear the whole stadium was shaking, and it probably was. When I went back to man my position for the next batter, I felt bad for Tom—all of us did. Perfect games are rare, and to be part of one to that point was a feeling I'll never forget. The score was 4–0, but things like that can shake up a pitcher. Still, Tom didn't let it get to him. Willie Smith popped out next, and Kessinger flied out to me for the final out of the game—a lazy fly ball similar to the one Qualls hit but this time right at me.

When I made that last catch, I thought about what it means to throw a perfect game, everything that needs to happen to achieve one. Certainly the more strikeouts a pitcher gets, the better chance he has. And we'd been taught all the way from the sandlot on up to put the ball in play because you never know what will happen.

Qualls's fly ball was no better or worse than the one Kessinger hit, but it was perfectly placed—by luck or good fortune—but both seemed to be following us all year long.

The Seaver game was another in a season full of so much emotion and tension. Tom had lost his perfect game, but more importantly it had pulled us to within 3½ of the Cubs. It energized and motivated us. But after Tom lost a heartbreaking, 1–0 game just five days later in Chicago, we fell behind by six games. It seemed like every time we got close, Chicago would open up their lead again. We kept chasing and they kept staying ahead.

Two months had passed, and we had another chance to gain on the Cubs. We beat them in the first game of a two-game series and pulled to within 1½ games. I wanted to be back in the lineup, despite the fact I had cracked a few ribs and hadn't played in a week. I hadn't homered since late July, but I was still getting my hits and my batting average had stayed above .340 all that time, so Gil penciled me in. I had never felt such an energy as I did that night at Shea Stadium—even more so than the night of Seaver's near perfect game. And after Tom set down the order in the first inning, we went right to work. Agee walked and so did I. And as it had been happening all season long, another hero—Wayne Garrett—doubled to right, scoring both Tommie and myself for a 2–0 lead. That was all Seaver needed.

But what happened in the Cubs' fourth inning has gone down in Mets folklore for all this time. Some people said it was a sign—an omen—when a black cat simply showed up on the field, walked behind the on-deck circle where Ron Santo stood, and starting parading in front of the Cubs dugout as if it had been rehearsed.

It was amazing in the sense that this black cat walked in front of Leo Durocher and seemed to pause and look at him. That black cat seemed to have bothered Leo, and he didn't move at all for those few seconds. Leo was a good manager—no doubt about it—but everybody could think of something they didn't like about him. When the black cat showed up, that was a sign in many people's minds that something was about to happen in terms of luck, and it was being directed at the right person. Had it been an ordinary game or early on in the season and a black cat came out onto the field, it may have been noted, but a big deal wouldn't have been made. But of all games and of all series, with the first-place Cubs barely holding onto first place, it made for an extremely tense situation. It felt like a must-win game at the time.

To this day I don't know where that black cat came from. I had never seen a black cat in the ballpark before. I don't know if somebody brought the cat into the stadium or he crossed the interstate to get into the stadium. I never saw a cat under the stands, in the locker room, or even outside the ballpark. We saw pigeons and other birds on the field but never a cat on the field. And it wasn't just a cat—it was a black cat.

It was comical to us because the game was delayed as they were trying to get the cat off the field. That put more focus on the cat because he had to be removed from the field, and so the concentration from all the players, all the people in the stands, and the TV was on that cat. So that was a defining moment right there.

Everybody has their thoughts about it being an omen because we were on a roll and the Cubs were sliding. I'm not sure if any of the Cubs players were superstitious or not, but it was a moment to think about such things. Ernie had something to say about everything regarding how good the Cubs were, and he said, "Who put that black cat out there? We don't care about no black cat, we're baseball players. We're winners... where did that cat come from?"

We pulled to within a half game of the Cubs that night, with yet another doubleheader set the next night with the Expos. The opener against Montreal was a 3–2, 12-inning affair with Ken Boswell the latest Mets hero. It was another tight pitcher's duel between Jim McAndrew and the Expos' Mike Wegener, with both of them pitching 11 strong innings before giving way to the bullpens in the 12th. Jim had come on strong at the end of the year when we needed it most, winning three straight nine-inning starts in late August over which time he allowed just two runs total, including two shutouts against the Giants and Padres. He deserved to win against the Expos, but Wegener was pitching like he had against us earlier in April when he lost to us 2–1. For some reason we had our troubles against him.

Some people had started saying we were getting lucky because of the way we'd been winning games and that our luck was bound to change. But in a season full of games that mostly went our way, we scored a run on a balk that tied the game 2–2 in the fifth. Balks are one of those things you rarely see in a game, let alone one that gives you a run. That may sound lucky to some—and maybe it was—but it happened and happened at just the right time.

We were trailing 2–1 in our half of the fifth when Harrelson popped out and McAndrew struck out. Agee was coming up next, and we knew with one swing of the bat he could tie it up. Tommie didn't hit one out, but after he reached on an error, he went to third on a single by Wayne Garrett. Wegener then walked me to load the bases, bringing Art Shamsky to the plate. That's when Wegener committed a balk, and the game was tied.

There's an old adage in baseball to never give the other team more than three outs in an inning because that's when bad things happen. I've seen that many times before. And look what happened. Two outs and nobody on base, and we scored a run on an error, a single, a walk, and a balk. You never know in this game what's going to happen next, and what happened in that inning was a microcosm of our season.

That inning kind of got lost in memorable moments of the season, but not to me. We kept trying to scrape out a run, and this one was an example of all that. Two outs and nobody on base never left us feeling we couldn't score. Gil always felt that way, and we believed in him and in each other. That we won it in the 12th with two outs and nobody on base was more proof of that. It looked like the game would go to the 13th after Bill Stoneman got Agee to fly to right and struck out Garrett. But I singled to center, Gaspar walked, and Boswell sent me home with a single to center for the winning run.

The Cubs had a game in Philadelphia that night with our second game of the doubleheader coming up. We had actually gone into first place with that win—one percentage point over the Cubs—and the fans were celebrating. We were happy and feeling good about things, but the chase of the Cubs, which had lasted all year wasn't over at game 140. Sometimes when you're chasing for so long, there might be a letdown at some point, but we'd been resilient all season long and knew it was far too early for any celebrating to be going on. We still had 22 more games to play.

We sent 10 men to the plate against the Expos in the third inning of Game 2 and scored six runs. That gave Nolan Ryan all the breathing room he needed. Nolan pitched a complete game, giving up just three hits while striking out 11 in our 7–1 win. We could already see how dominant he could be, but he'd had blisters most of the season. He had some spot starts here and there and was used out of the bullpen most the time, but I knew he could be a full-time starter.

While we were winning the second game of our doubleheader, the Phillies rallied in the seventh to tie their game with the Cubs, then scored three runs off of Phil Regan in the eighth to win it. It was another case of Leo overusing Regan, who didn't retire a batter in the inning. I knew it would catch up to them sooner or later—and it was one of the reasons we all felt we were going to win the division. Despite all the doubleheaders still to play, our pitching depth seemed far deeper than that of the reeling Cubs. The scoreboard in right field at Shea said it all. We were in first place by a full game over the Cubs with 21 to play.

We won four more in a row after that, giving us a 10-game winning streak before losing to the Pirates. It had been our second such streak of 10 wins or more, and with the Cubs continuing to lose, we fattened our lead to 3½ games going into St. Louis.

All of New York seemed to be going crazy by now. The season had just 16 games left, and the talk was no longer about us winning our division, but lots of folks started talking about who we'd face in the playoffs. All that was just talk to me. I was just trying to heal and hoped to be ready as soon as I could. I sat out 10 games during that stretch run, including the first game in St. Louis after we took over first place. The Cardinals had long fallen out of the race after making an earlier run, but they'd always played us tough and had their young lefty Steve Carlton on the mound. Carlton had good stuff, and we could see he could be among the best in the game. We'd faced him three times that season, and we struck out a lot against him.

But I'd had good success off of Carlton, going 4-for-7 with no strikeouts. It didn't matter and never did to me who was pitching that game or the next one, and I knew I could help the club with a guy like Carlton on the mound. But being unable to play, other guys—like we'd done all year long—had to step up. Most of the time during the year it wouldn't be just one guy doing all the damage in any one game. Whether it was a pitcher or a batter or a great defensive play, there were multiple players contributing on a nightly basis—three or four guys with an RBI, a great game by a starting pitcher, or a fantastic relief job from the bullpen. That was the fun of the season, really, because we didn't know game to game who would be that game's hero.

The next guy to step up was Ron Swoboda. Ronnie had struggled against Carlton and was struggling of late, batting .195 for September (8-for-41) and striking out a lot (15 Ks in 41 at-bats). From what I remember, Ronnie went to our broadcaster, Ralph Kiner, to get some hitting tips. We didn't have any batting coaches back then, so from time to time guys would rely on some outside source to help them out, to see if maybe they noticed something about their swing or stance, and seeing as Ralph was a former slugger and home-run champion, as well as a keen observer from the broadcast booth, it was worth a try.

It didn't start out well for Ron or the team as Carlton ended the first inning striking out Ron and two others. Carlton again stuck out the side in the second inning and had seven strike-outs when Ron came to bat in the fourth. Carlton had walked Donn Clendenon to start the inning, and then Ron hit a two-run homer to give us a 2–1 lead.

Carlton was racking up strikeouts, but we were getting on base against him. After Swoboda's home run, Carlton gave up a single and then struck out the side again to give him 10 Ks for the game. Considering Buddy had gotten picked off first by Carlton in the third, our only batted out to this point was a pop fly by Amos Otis, and in a season of the improbable, we were still ahead in the game.

The Cardinals took the lead back in the fifth on four straight singles from Lou Brock, Curt Flood, Vada Pinson, and Joe Torre, making it 3–2 St. Louis. Then Carlton got out of trouble in the seventh. By that time he'd chalked up 14 strikeouts and was in range of the all-time record of 18 set by Bob Feller and tied by Sandy Koufax and Don Wilson. But when Swoboda connected for another two-run homer in the eighth, we took the lead for good and won the game 4–3.

Of course, Carlton ended up breaking the strikeout record when he fanned five more guys in the final two innings for a total of 19, but he had to have had mixed feelings about it. It was unusual for a pitcher to strike out that many batters and lose the game, unusual for it not be as dominating as it sounds. Around all those strikeouts, we put a lot of men on base, and it was Swoboda's only two–home run game of the season. With the Cubs losing to Montreal, we picked up another game and led by 4½.

We slipped a little after that historic game. We took two from the Expos in Montreal and then dropped three to the Pirates at home. But the Cubs' late-season collapse continued, and they only managed to pick up a game on us during those three losses to Pittsburgh. We finally clinched our division at home less than a week later on a four-hit shutout by Gary Gentry and a three-run homer by Donn Clendenon and a solo homer by Ed Charles in the first inning off of that same Steve Carlton. It's funny how baseball can be. Carlton had 19 strikeouts against us just a week earlier, and now he was pulled after recording just one out.

We were jubilant, ecstatic—all the adjectives you can throw out there describe the clubhouse that night. But while we had cinched our division, Atlanta and San Francisco were still battling it out in the NL West, and it looked like it was coming down to the wire.

Theirs was more of a classic pennant chase than ours was—at least in the final two weeks of the season—with both teams winning night after night. The Giants had swept the Braves in a two-game series at Candlestick, led the Braves by just a half game, and after a loss to Houston won five in a row. But the Braves were hotter and won 10 straight. Judging by all their double-digit scoring totals, their offense was in high gear.

Before the Braves clinched, people were asking us whom we'd rather play. But you can't say who that is. Everyone knows you can't give the other team any extra motivation, and you have to give answers that respect both teams. And even though the Braves were scoring at will and were as hot as we'd been, with a short series and looking at how the pitching lined up, I think most of us would have rather played the Braves.

Of course, we had great respect for Phil Niekro (23–13) and Ron Reed (18–10), as well as Pat Jarvis (13–11) and George Stone (13–10). But the Giants had Juan Marichal (21–11), Gaylord Perry

(19–14), and Mike McCormick (11–9), and all three were tougher to hit.

During the season, we'd had success against Niekro every time we faced him and probably would be facing him twice if the series went five games. Niekro threw that knuckleball, and when he was on, it was hard to hit. Reed seemed to give us more trouble than Niekro did, but Marichal and Perry were a harder duo to deal with back-to-back.

Marichal was right up there with guys like Koufax and Gibson, so having to face him a couple times could be difficult. He was tough as nails and never wanted to come out of a game. He was on the losing side of that epic game in August when Agee homered off him in the 14th inning. Juan came back on us just a few days later and shut us out out on four hits. Knowing what he'd done against us and that over a short series he'd probably be going up against Seaver, with Perry versus Koosman, the games would undoubtedly become pitchers' duels, though we'd handled that task all season long.

We did better off of Gaylord Perry, but he was a veteran and had been through it before. Again, it's funny sometimes how a player and a team performs against certain guys, and I know I struggled against him. But the team responded better against Perry, and that was more important.

But none of that mattered. We'd gone 8–4 against both teams in the regular season, but it wouldn't have mattered if we'd won all 24 games because it all goes out the window with the playoffs. Look at how poor our record was against Houston (2–10)—we knew that any team in the league was capable of winning a five-game series.

Both teams had some pretty explosive offensive threats, be it the Braves' Hank Aaron, Orlando Cepeda, and Rico Carty, or the Giants' Willie Mays, Willie McCovey, and Bobby Bonds. What

I'd learned from Casey Stengel early in my career was to have your pitching staff concentrate more on the other hitters in their lineup, because those players would usually do some damage. Aaron had his usual super year (44 HRs, 97 RBIs); Cepeda could hit with the best of the them (22 HRs, 88 RBIs); and Carty was always a .300 hitter (.342). Willie Mays's production had slipped for a few years (13 HRs, 58 RBIs), but he was Willie Mays, and you knew what he could do. McCovey had become a true super-star with back-to-back seasons leading the league in home runs and RBIs (45 HRs, 126 RBIs), and Bonds (32 HRs, 90 RBIs) was a rising star with power and speed. But any thinking about who our opponent was going to be started to clear up when the Braves won 10 straight around the same time we had, and they pulled away and finally clinched it near the end.

I liked playing in Atlanta. It was a good hitter's park with a good background. If I had a place that I'd rather play, it would be Atlanta and Chicago—both hitter's parks. And Chicago and Atlanta were usually hot—the way I like it.

We went into Atlanta for the first game with Seaver on the mound against Niekro, but Tom wasn't his sharpest and gave up a go-ahead homer to Aaron in the seventh to make it 5–4 Braves. After Wayne Garrett led off the eighth with a double, I came up with the chance to tie the game with a single. I was finally feeling comfortable at the plate for the first time since my injury and had had two good at-bats earlier against Niekro with no results. But I was just seeing the ball better, and when that happens you have more confidence as a hitter. I was back to the mindset that it didn't matter who was pitching—I was attacking my hitting zone and seeing the ball well, and knew I was starting to get my stroke back. I singled to tie the game, went to second on a single by Shamsky, stole third, and came home with the go-ahead run on Kranepool's grounder to first and an errant throw home by Cepeda.

We'd taken advantage of opportunities like that all season long—errors by our opponents that extended a rally and good managing when it was needed most. When the Braves intentionally walked Buddy to load the bases, we knew it was to face Seaver at the plate, but Gil sent in J.C. Martin to pinch-hit, and just like we'd done all year with a line of new heroes every game, J.C. cleared the bases with a single to right and another Braves error, giving us a five-run inning and a 9–5 lead. Ron Taylor recorded the final six outs, and we took Game 1.

The Braves were a little shocked at how the game ended, and we were happy we'd supported Seaver when he wasn't at his best. Tom hadn't had a game like that since early August in Cincinnati. But then he dominated the rest of the way, so we were somewhat surprised.

With the Braves having such a dominant right-handed lineup, we were hoping Koosman would give us what we'd been used to down the stretch in Game 2. Hardly anybody had an offensive unit like Atlanta did, and it wasn't just Aaron, Cepeda, and Carty. Clete Boyer, Felipe Alou, and Felix Millan all could hit, and all six guys were right-handed batters. We felt like Atlanta was a good offensive unit, a professional team in every sense of the word, and that we had to score runs because they were going to score with a potent lineup like that.

We stayed hot in Game 2 in Atlanta and scored in each of the first five innings for a commanding 9–1 lead. Atlanta cut the lead to 9–6 with a big rally in the fifth to chase Koosman, and it stayed that way until I came up in the seventh with Tommie on third base. I really felt like I had got my stroke back, getting two hits earlier in the game and knocking in one. I was in the same groove I was in when I was batting around .360, and with Tommie on third, I had a chance to put the game away with just a single.

Then I saw Tommie coming down the line, trying to steal home, and I fouled one off. So I stepped out of the box, looked toward him, and said, "Just hold on a minute, I'll get you in." And two pitches later, I hit a home run just like I said, giving us an 11–6 lead. From there, Ron Taylor and Tug closed the door with great relief pitching, and we were up 2–0 on our way back home for the rest of the series.

We fell behind in the first inning of Game 3 when Aaron homered for the third time in the series—a long home run to dead-center—and I started thinking about what Casey had said about the superstars as Hank trotted around the bases. We hadn't really shut down the rest of their lineup like we expected to, but they were more surprised by the offense we'd displayed in the first two games. Now they were hoping that Pat Jarvis would be sharp and be able to shut us down.

But our offense stayed in full gear with home runs by Agee, Boswell, and Garrett, and Nolan Ryan pitched seven strong innings in relief of Gentry. When the Braves' Tony Gonzalez grounded to third base for the final out, we'd won the series in a sweep, and it was bedlam in New York.

We'd scored 27 runs in three games, batted .327 as a team, and belted six home runs—something we hadn't done all year in any three-game stretch. And because we'd faced all right-handers, two of our power hitters—Donn Clendenon and Ron Swoboda— didn't even come to the plate the entire series.

I hit .429 in the series, with a homer and four RBIs, but so many guys had a terrific series at the plate—Art Shamsky, Wayne Garrett, Tommie Agee, Ken Boswell, and I all had at least four hits each and accounted for all six of our home runs. We'd made believers out of Atlanta, and now it was Baltimore's turn.

Chapter 12

BALTIMORE

THERE WAS LITTLE time to celebrate our win against the Braves. The Orioles had swept the Twins, but it wasn't that easy. A couple of extra-inning games and a blowout gave them the series.

We kept getting reminders from some of those same writers and experts who pegged us for last place or next-to-last place in our division. During the season, before we made our surge toward the end, our detractors quickly had us faltering down the stretch and gave us little chance against the Cubs or Cardinals. Even after we won our division, most of the experts had us losing to the Braves. And now that we had swept them, they gave us little chance against the mighty Baltimore Orioles in the World Series.

On paper, it was a mismatch across most of the positions but pretty even with the pitching. Their offense began with Frank Robinson, who'd already won an MVP in both leagues and the triple crown a few years earlier. Add in Boog Powell, Brooks Robinson, and my old buddy Paul Blair, and those four guys alone hit more home runs than we did as a team. Their top two pitchers—Mike Cuellar and Dave McNally—were similar to Seaver and Koosman, and those would likely be the matchups for at least the first two games of the Series.

But we had something the Orioles hadn't had all year, and that was the struggle. We had battled back all season long chasing the Cubs, but Baltimore had breezed though their division, going into first place in April and stretching their lead into double-digits by the end of June. At no time after that were they threatened or hit a slump.

A team with such a big lead can get complacent near the end of the season, and while we were riding a 10-game winning streak at the end, they ended by losing five of six and not scoring much. Of course, Earl Weaver was resting some of his starters, but it's not the way a team wants to finish after dominating all season long. But all that went out the window as we went into Baltimore for the first two games of the Series. All the regular-season statistics or winning streaks or losing streaks meant nothing at all.

Going into Game 1, I wanted to get off to a good start with my first at-bat. I'd felt good against Atlanta and wanted to keep it going. My first at-bat in a World Series was single off of Cuellar in the first inning, and what a feeling that was. I wasn't thinking about such things at all, but I became the first Met in history to get a hit in a World Series, something I was proud of later on. There was no big deal made of it, but inside I almost felt like a kid again getting a hit in a World Series game. We didn't score and took the field with Seaver on the mound.

The Braves had hit Tom pretty well in Atlanta, but with a full week of rest, we felt confident he'd bounce back. But one player the Orioles had that I didn't mention earlier was Don Buford. With a roster full of stars, Buford's name always seemed to be mentioned in that next tier of good players. He was a good lead-off hitter, drawing walks, getting singles, that sort of thing. He had some pop in his bat, but we didn't expect him to hit one out as the first batter to face Seaver.

Buford took Tom's second pitch deep to right, and I thought Ron Swoboda had a chance to catch the ball when it left the bat.

Ron made routine fly balls exciting at times because you were never sure if he knew where the ball was. I watched him sort of circle around on Buford's fly and slowly start to go back to the wall like he had a bead on it. Then when he made his leap, I thought he'd come down with it, but he just missed it. The very first batter the Mets had ever faced in the World Series had homered.

We fell behind 4–0 when five straight Orioles batters reached base in the fourth, including a Mike Cuellar single that drove in a run. Like most pitchers, Cuellar wasn't much of a hitter. In later years I discovered he had only five RBIs all season and hit just over .100. That brought up once again what Casey had always preached to us, that the superstars would get their hits, you just had to control the others. To have guys like Buford and Cuellar driving in half their runs certainly that wasn't a very good sign at all.

Seaver certainly didn't have his best stuff, but we had a good chance in the seventh when we loaded the bases against Cuellar. But all we could manage was one run on a sac fly from Al Weis and didn't threaten after that. The experts were looking pretty good at the time. Some said we'd lose in four or five games, but nobody was saying we'd win. Nobody except Rod Gaspar.

Rod had gone on national TV and said we'd sweep the Orioles. We certainly didn't want to give Baltimore any extra incentive, as that kind of thing often comes back to haunt you. Some of the Orioles really took what he said to heart. Frank Robinson responded by saying, "Bring on the Mets and Ron Gaspar!" Merv Rettenmund, one of Frank's teammates, said, "It's Rod, stupid." Then Frank said, "Okay. Bring on Rod Stupid!"

I don't know if Rod was taken out of context for what he said, and the one thing I didn't do was read the papers or the columns or watch the news because I was there and I knew what we were doing. I recall that what Rod had said was going around, and we were reminded by some Baltimore fans when some of us went out to dinner after that game.

There was a bunch of us together that night, including Seaver, Koosman, Agee, and others. There was some guy sitting over from us bragging that Baltimore was going to sweep us, that the Mets didn't have any business being on the same field with Baltimore, and that they were the greatest team since the 1927 Yankees. They went on and on, and I don't remember who said something to the guy, but I think it was Seaver who asked the guy if he wanted to make a bet on it. This guy had been really loud, and for some reason I don't think he had any idea who we were at that point. Then he said in a sort of defensive tone, "What?" And while he looked at us, some others around him told him who we were. The guy just smiled, said he didn't want to make a bet, and the conversation went on for a while with some more good-natured ribbing. Nobody got out of line, it was just fans being fans and wanting their team to win. All the ribbing and all the predictions from all the naysayers didn't get us down. When you were as confident as we were, the loss of one game didn't diminish our attitude. We didn't feel down because we knew there was tomorrow, and we'd bounced back all year long.

But winning a game in Baltimore was on our minds as we prepared for Game 2. Everyone knew all the math and all the history surrounding teams going down two games to none, but again, I paid that kind of thing no mind at all. All I knew was we had to win at least one game at their park if we were going to win the whole thing, and they really dominated at home, going 60–21 during the season.

Before our first game loss, Clendenon hadn't played in almost 10 days and was champing at the bit to get in. With Atlanta throwing nothing but righties against us in the playoffs, Donn sat while Kranepool played first—always a tough thing for a player to not partake in any of it. But Donn showed no signs of being rusty when he homered off of Dave McNally in the fourth inning of Game 2 to give us a 1–0 lead.

Meanwhile, Koosman was his usual self to that point—even better than usual—and had a no-hitter going after six. But Paul Blair led off the seventh with a single to ruin his bid, stole second, and scored on a clutch two-out single from Brooks Robinson to tie the game 1–1. This was the kind of game we'd gotten used to playing all season long, and the score stayed that way into the ninth when three more heroes came through for us.

It looked like another one-two-three inning for McNally when Clendenon struck out and Swoboda grounded out, but we'd rallied before under those same conditions and would do it again. Ed Charles and Jerry Grote both singled, and our little mighty-might of the series, Al Weis, broke the tie with another single that scored Charles from third.

I believe McNally was somewhat surprised at all that. Here was a bona fide, Cy Young Award–caliber pitcher giving up key hits to three guys all batting under .250, with two of them closer to .200. There couldn't have been many times during the season McNally gave up three hits in a row like that, and now he was getting a taste of just who we were, and who we'd been all season long.

It was looking good for us when Koosman retired the first two batters in the bottom of the ninth. But after he walked Frank Robinson and Boog Powell, Gil Hodges brought in Ron Taylor to get the last out. Ron got Brooks Robinson to ground to third, and we'd done what we set out to do—earned a split with Baltimore on their field.

Chapter 13

WORLD SERIES GAMES 3–5

COMING HOME TO SHEA for the next three games of the Series certainly gave us the advantage we were looking for. Of course, we had to take one game at a time, but we all knew that, win or lose, those next three games would be the last three games at Shea Stadium in 1969. We also knew we'd have to win all three games for our fans to celebrate with us at home. Certainly that was a tall order, but we felt we could do it. Our fans and all of New York were so full of energy and enthusiasm, and other things were happening around the ballpark that motivated us even more for the fans.

We always had to deal with distractions at the ballpark, but I'd learned long before to tune it all out. Between fans asking for autographs, others calling you names, and reporters asking questions, you had to learn to ignore some stuff and not let any of those things get to you. After a while, you got used to it and just concentrated on yourself and what you needed to do to help the team win, because if you didn't find a way to block it all out, it took away your focus.

The jets flying in and out of LaGuardia were so frequent, I got to the point that I didn't look up anymore. I knew during the course of a ballgame there'd be jets flying, sometimes every inning. Some things I got so attuned to that they became a part of my rhythm. To the point that I'd get worried when I didn't hear jets flying overhead. It was just routine. It was just part of the scene for our home games, and it never bothered me. But there were some fun distractions unique to Shea Stadium that began with our organ player, Jane Jarvis, and "Sign Man" Karl Ehrhardt.

Both of them had been at Shea since I'd come up to the team, so they were part of the fabric and the ambiance surrounding the ballpark. Jane set the tone before the game even started, and Karl set the tone during the game. It was a sort of one-two punch of quality entertainment that made the experience better for the fans and the players. Jane always played, "Let's Go, Mets," before we took the field for our home games, getting the fans into it before a pitch was even thrown. She had a knack for playing songs that were just right for the moment and was good at entertaining the fans throughout the game. Karl set the tone during games with his signs, so there was more going on around us than just a ballgame.

Karl evidently was a magician in his own right, because practically anything that happened on the field he had an answer to—good, bad, or indifferent. He had a sign that referenced what had just taken place, and he had it out almost immediately after it had happened on the field. It seemed like he had dozens, maybe hundreds, of signs organized in a portfolio that he had right next to him, but he always drew out the perfect sign. I know there was a lot of thought that went into all that.

He sat behind third base to the left of the visitors' dugout, and I had a great view of him when he posted his signs. It was amazing how he knew where everything was. He was part of the action because whenever something good happened for us, he'd post it and people would applaud. He was our 10th man. I had a conversation with him briefly, applauding him for all of his efforts and for lugging that equipment to the stadium for every home game. He certainly was part of every inning and every out in every situation that took place on the field, and having him there was one of those unique things about the Mets and playing at Shea. I heard he was still going strong into the early '80s, and his collection of signs for all those years amounted to more than 1,000.

With Jane and Karl providing so much entertainment at our home games, another of those fun distractions that we all looked forward to was the annual "Banner Day" at Shea. It was a fun day for everyone, and a a spectacle you just didn't see at any other ballpark. It's hard to imagine all the things you witnessed that day that were printed or painted on a sheet. It just goes to show you how much people put into being a fan and expressing themselves. And there were some signs on that day that were mind-blowing. As players, we valued our time between batting practice and outfield practice, but we all found ourselves in the dugout watching what was going on, reading the great ideas people came with—putting them on canvas and marching around the field with smiles on their faces, just being elated about taking part in what was a one-of-a-kind event at Shea. Maybe they did it at other ballparks, but not on this scale.

We interacted with some of the fans who paraded around the field because it was a special day for the them, but it was a special day for all of us. When people walked by, we waved and hollered and made some comments. I had my favorites, but I can't recall what they were because so many were so clever that they made me laugh. I imagine all of Shea—all of the workers, management, grounds crews, even the general manager—watched this because it was that special.

With all the fun that the Mets provided with our organist, our Sign Man, and a day for the fans with Banner Day, there was something else that featured a player or two after every home game on a show they called *Kiner's Korner*.

After any home win, Ralph would invite a player or two on to talk about the game and what he did to help win it. Like everything else, I'd never been that excited about talking about myself, but you had to if you were a guest on *Kiner's Korner*. In 1969 I'd become a guest so often on his show, I remember them saying they should change the name to "Cleon's Corner."

They'd bring us on to the set right after the game was over, and we'd still be in uniform. Ralph had his notes, and they had a TV monitor replaying any highlights he wanted to talk about. Of course, he wanted to talk about you because you were his invited guest. But I'd always been more comfortable having other folks talking about me and not touting my own victories and my own achievements. I always said I don't read about myself and I don't like talking about myself. I've always been that way, I guess.

You're always thinking about your teammates and how you can win ballgames and how you can be a plus in crucial situations. We won the game. It takes a team to lose, and it takes a team to win. I may have made an error earlier in the game, and maybe I came up and had a big hit later that put us in front. I'd rather be talking about the guys who got on base who made it possible for me to drive them in. Even in high school, I talked about everybody else. When people mentioned me breaking records, I tried focusing on other teammates. It was never my goal to set a record or break a record. I was focused on what was at hand—the game and winning. It didn't matter who scored the winning touchdown or who made the final basket to win the game. It was always, in my mind, a team effort.

But Ralph had a way that put us at ease and allowed us to talk about our teammates. He always asked the right questions, likely because he was an exciting player who hit a lot of home runs and understood sharing the importance of his success with his teammates. Some people in the media might have said, "You hit a home run, but it wasn't a very good pitch." Ralph never got off like that. He knew hitting home runs wasn't easy, and always leaned on the positive. He always made you feel at ease and asked the right questions as it related to me. Ralph Kiner was a baseball icon to me and to most of us because he was a star in his own right. He wasn't in the Hall of Fame yet, but I looked at him as if he were. He'd hit almost 400 home runs and was an All-Star for several years. Ralph was one of the greats of the game. It was a privilege being in the same room with him talking about baseball.

The entire Mets media staff that we had was just outstanding. Kiner, Bob Murphy, and Lindsay Nelson were real pros. They had a knack for making you feel at ease and saying all the right things. Even when they walked by you, they had a way that made you smile and feel good about yourself.

With all the marketing and interactions with Mets fans, none of it ever distracted us. We all knew when to enjoy such things, but never did it alter our focus. But now, going into Game 3, we all wanted a seat on *Kiner's Korner.*

We were going with Gary Gentry for Game 3 against Jim Palmer, a good matchup of two righties. Palmer was another of those tough Baltimore starters, but Gary was on a roll. We knew Gary had good stuff right at the start of the season, but he wasn't supposed to be our No. 3 starter that year—Nolan was. But Nolan had blister problems during the year. Gary took his place in the rotation and found his groove in September. It didn't seem like we gave Gary a lot of run support during the season, but during the stretch run, that seemed to have changed for the better.

Game 3 certainly belonged to Tommie Agee, both at the plate and on defense. And like Buford had done to Seaver in Game 1, Tommie took Palmer deep to center leading off the first inning, and just like that, we led 1–0.

The Series became known for its great catches by our outfielders, and all that began in the Orioles' fourth when Tommie ran a mile to left-center to rob Ellie Hendricks of a two-run double. When I played center field at Shea, I wasn't fond of it because it was tough to pick up the ball with so many people wearing white shirts. But Agee had no problem at all with that. He went back to the wall and made a back-handed catch, and I could see about half the ball sticking out of his glove. It was tremendous catch that saved two runs.

By the seventh we'd stretched our lead to 4–0 on Gary Gentry's two-run double in the second inning and another run-scoring double by Jerry Grote. We'd seen Jerry drive in some key runs, but nobody was expecting Gary to produce. Gary had hit under .100 for the season and fanned about 70 percent of the time. He'd only had a few hits and drove in just one run the whole year. But when he took Palmer deep to right-center on the first pitch, it was another of those amazing moments in an unending line of them.

A lot of folks talked about all the great catches and the shoe-polish game when the series was over, but for me, that double was just as important. The Orioles' outfield had played him so shallow, it was good too see him drive one over their heads in such surprising fashion, and it probably demoralized Palmer because he likely wasn't too concerned with Gary, and that's understandable. But baseball is full of surprises, and we had more to come.

But Gary walked three straight batters in the seventh after getting the first two batters, and that's when Gil brought in Nolan Ryan to face Paul Blair. Blair nailed one to right-center, and Tommie took off again, falling to the ground with another great catch—this one saving three runs. Like Hendricks earlier, Blair turned back and could hardly believe it as he went back to the dugout. We won that game 5–0 and now held a 2–1 Series lead.

All the talk centered on Tommie Agee and for good reason. Two great catches saving five runs and a home run tends to get you into the headlines. Those catches changed the course of the game, but I'd been right next to him all year and seen him make catches like those all the time. But when you do it on a stage of that magnitude in the World Series, everything is magnified. We were there because we'd been making plays like that all year, taking runs from our opponents, doing all the right things so you don't beat yourself, making the right throws, hitting the cut-off man, and being a complete team. I wasn't surprised Tommie made those catches because that's what he did. The bigger surprise for me would have been if he hadn't made them.

But in Game 4 the catch of the game didn't come from Tommie, it came from Ron Swoboda—our most unlikely candidate to do so. We had Seaver going again, and he looked like the Tom Seaver we'd been used to seeing all year. Clendenon hit his second homer of the Series off of Mike Cuellar in the second and our 1–0 lead held into the ninth. Tom seemed to be in complete control. When Frank Robinson and Boog Powell singled, they had men on first and third with one out when the play of the Series happened.

Brooks Robinson hit a lazy fly ball to right, and from my vantage point it was going to fall in for a hit—especially with Swoboda charging after the ball. Swoboda had been working hard on his defense all year, and I'd seen him trying to make a play like that for years and never get to one. Ronnie took hundreds of sinking fly balls from the coaches and never caught even one. He had practiced for that exact play, constantly asking the coaches to hit ones to him again and again. It got to the point that they hoped he wouldn't ask so much so they could take a break. It's

Cleon Jones with the New York Mets on May 12, 1969, posing with an assortment of his bats while fans look on. After that day's doubleheader with the Houston Astros, Cleon was batting .411. He ended up hitting .340 for the season and led the Mets to their first World Series title that October.

Cleon (above) robs the Cubs' Paul Popovich of a hit at Wrigley Field in Chicago on the last game of the regular season, October 1, 1969. • In Game 1 of the 1969 NLCS in Atlanta (below), Cleon slides into home plate to put the Mets up 6–5 over the Braves in the eighth inning. The Mets scored three more runs in the inning and held on to win 9–5.

The Mets' Tommie Agee (above) makes a great running catch against the Baltimore Orioles' Ellie Hendricks in Game 3 of the 1969 World Series, with Cleon backing up the play. • Umpire Lou DiMuro (below) awards Cleon (21) first base after manager Gil Hodges showed him the shoe polish on the ball, a pivotal moment in Game 5 in New York.

Seven members of the world champion 1969 New York Mets entertain at Caesar's Palace in Las Vegas (from left): Art Shamsky, Tommie Agee, Tom Seaver, Donn Clendenon, Ed Kranepool, Jerry Koosman, and Cleon Jones. They're singing "The Impossible Dream" to a sellout crowd on November 7, 1969.

Cleon in St. Petersburg, Florida, with the Mets for spring training in March 1971.

Manager Yogi Berra (above, 8) talks with recently injured Mets (from left) Cleon, John Milner, and Rusty Staub in the locker room at Shea Stadium in July 1972. • In Game 1 of the 1973 World Series (below), Cleon slides into home plate, scoring one of the Mets' four runs in the sixth inning of their 12-inning, 10–7 win over the Oakland A's.

Cleon with his wife, Angela, and son, Cleon Jr., in the dugout at Shea Stadium for Mets Family Day on July 19, 1975, the day after Cleon refused to take left field after being given no time by manager Yogi Berra to put on his knee brace, which he needed to play due to a knee injury. The Mets released him later that month.

Cleon standing next to his jersey at the Mobile County Training School Whippets Alumni Den in Africatown, where he and Angela attended high school (it's now a middle school). *Photo courtesy of Cleon Jones*

Cleon with Hank Aaron at a dedication ceremony at Hank Aaron Stadium in Mobile, Alabama.
Photo courtesy of Cleon Jones

New York City mayor Bill de Blasio poses with Cleon after presenting him with a key to the city on June 29, 2019, in New York.

This aerial photo from 2018 shows the remains of what would later be confirmed to be the *Clotilda*, the last known ship to have delivered enslaved Africans to the U.S., illegally in 1860. Local journalist Ben Raines discovered the wreck in the Mobile River off of 12-Mile Island. Survivors of the wreck founded Africatown.

From left to right, back row: Anja (daughter), Cleon, Anjelica (granddaughter), Albert (grandson), and Cleon Jr. *Middle row*: Angela, Morgan (granddaughter), Myles (grandson), and Natalie (daughter-in-law). *Front row*: Autumn (great-granddaughter) and Joshua (grandson). *Photo courtesy of Cleon Jones*

as if he knew that one day he'd be in that very position to make that catch.

When he dove and came up with the ball off of Brooks Robinson's bat, it was truly one of the greatest catches that I'd seen anybody make. He dove for that ball, and if he hadn't come up with it, they'd have been running forever.

He was a guy who was probably one of the worst outfielders in baseball early on in his career. But he never stopped working to get better, and at that point in time the work paid off for him. He used his judgment to go after that ball, and the way he went after it could have backfired.

Had that ball gotten by him, two runs would have scored, and Brooks Robinson could have ended up on third with one out and the lead. Not only did Ronnie prevent that with the catch, he came up with the right frame of mind to throw a rifle to home plate on Frank Robinson, who was tagging from third. He didn't get Frank, but he completed the play.

We entered the bottom of the ninth tied, with a chance to win it in our final at-bat. But the buzz around the stadium from that catch went on for a while. I singled and went to third when Swoboda singled me over, but Shamsky grounded out, and the game went into extra innings. Seaver worked out of a jam in the 10th, setting the scene for another improbable win.

Grote doubled to leadoff the inning and was replaced by pinch-runner Rod Gaspar. And in the cat-and-mouse games played by managers, Earl Weaver had Al Weis walked intentionally with Seaver coming up next, but Gil Hodges countered with J.C. Martin to pinch-hit for Seaver.

Gil had rolled the dice for us to win the game that inning. Our best defensive catcher and our best pitcher were out of the game, but we all knew from the moves Gil had made throughout the season that he liked the odds with two on and nobody out. When Weaver brought in lefty Pete Richert to face J.C., Gil walked out to the on-deck circle to talk with J.C. as Richert threw his warmup pitches. Nobody knew what Gil was saying at the time, but with men on first and second, the bunt certainly was in order.

On Richert's first pitch, J.C. laid down a soft bunt just past the dirt and onto the grass toward the first-base line. Ellie Hendricks and Richert almost collided when they both went for the ball, but Richert was the one who came up with it. I don't know if that slight hesitation made him hurry his throw, but he hit J.C. in the back with it, and Gaspar ran home with the winning run when the ball rolled toward second. You just can't even count the number of plays like that that went our way all year. We'd scored runs every way imaginable, and now on a throwing error to win a World Series game.

Despite a 3–1 Series lead, many of the experts thought Baltimore would come back and win, that we'd been lucky too much with great catches and weird endings like J.C.'s bunt and guys like Al Weis coming up with the big hit. There may be some luck in baseball, but it sure was good being on the right side of it. They had their opinions on all of that, but now that we'd won three straight, they said it was Baltimore's turn to do that.

I took a look around before Game 5, and it felt almost unbelievable we were on the verge of winning the World Series. But we knew the Orioles knew that, with one win at Shea, they'd go home for at least one more game. All our wishing to win the Series and to win it at home came down to this one game.

But Orioles starter Dave McNally hit a two-run homer off of Koosman in the third inning, and Frank Robinson followed with a solo blast a few outs later for an early 3–0 lead. Like Gary Gentry, McNally was hardly a threat at the plate, and Koosman probably overlooked him.

Then, with the score still 3–0 in the bottom of the sixth, the infamous "Shoe Polish" play started our rally.

We had already played in the "Black Cat" game against the Cubs, but never in a million years would I have thought some black shoe polish would change a game like it did this one. But it did. I led off the sixth against McNally, and he was shutting us down pretty well. I had good success off him in the minors when he was with Rochester, so I was looking for something good to drive. I'd really struggled in the Series with only a couple of hits and no RBIs, so I felt I was due and wanted to show them the player who'd batted .340 during the season.

He threw a slider down and in, and it hit me in the foot and bounced sideways into our dugout. After I got up off the ground, I made a move toward first base—I knew we needed base runners, but I was thinking bigger than that at the time and stayed outside the box when the home-plate umpire didn't make any kind of signal. Then Donn Clendenon started hollering from the on-deck circle, "The ball hit him!" He kept yelling that to the umpire, and I just stood there not knowing what to do. Clendenon kept shouting and pointing. Finally, Gil came out of the dugout carrying a ball and showed it to the umpire. A few seconds later, the umpire awarded me first base, and Gil walked back to the dugout.

Clendenon was our "clubhouse lawyer," and he was acting like it now. During the year he always spoke out and confronted most of us every day. He had something to say about every situation whether it be the game before or a game last week. If somebody had a good game, he'd say, "You were just lucky, let me see you do it again," that kind of thing. He was a clubhouse lawyer, but he was a motivator more than anything else.

He'd get on Grote and would make Grote mad, but he did it in a way that was team-oriented and about friendship, not about creating a barrier. He'd get on Kranepool and Shamsky a lot. He picked the people he did because it was his way of energizing the guys without them really knowing it, and I'm sot sure if he really knew he was doing it. It was easy for him to try and get on me because his locker was right next to mine. But I had figured him out long before everybody else figured him out, and I found him to be comical rather than annoying. He was always talking and always had something to say.

He was a veteran and had been around, so he knew how far he could take it when he joined the team. He knew everybody on the team because everybody who played against him at some point in time got to first base where had he something to say to them.

Ernie Banks spoke mostly about his players and how good they were and how good the team was and bragging about Billy Williams, Ron Santo being the best ever. Clendenon wasn't a promoter. He wasn't critical in the sense that he was trying to beat you down, he was trying to lift you up his way. We got on him all the time if he went 0-for-4 or had a bad game. But he'd just laugh and took it all in fun. He used criticism for fun.

The ball definitely hit me—it bounced clear into our dugout. Had that ball just hit the dirt, it never would have changed direction or bounced that far. Had here been no polishing of our shoes before the game, there would have been no evidence. All the Orioles were against the call, but I think McNally knew the ball hit me because of how it ricocheted. If the ball had missed me, it would have gone back behind home plate or off the catcher. Later on in the game, Frank Robinson was batting and claimed a ball hit him, but they didn't award him first base. The irony of the whole thing is that our clubhouse guy—Nick Torman—polished our shoes every day, and that may have made the difference.

I knew we were fighting for an opportunity for someone to get on base so we could get back in the game. I trotted down to first, and McNally looked a bit rattled, then Clendenon hit his third home run of the Series a few pitches later, and we were back in it, trailing 3–2.

When Al Weis homered to tie the game in the seventh, it was only his third of the season, and there was no doubt about it. Al proved to be quite a clutch player considering how he performed in all those doubleheader wins in the regular season and now with a game-tying home run in the World Series. He was a major league ballplayer, and I say that because he was a very capable middle infielder, able to put the bat on the ball all the time, so he wasn't an easy out.

Was I surprised when he hit that home run? Well, yes. You're surprised at most anything at that level when the non-starters are winning ballgames for you—that goes back to management making the right decisions on who could do the job for the team at a particular time. And that's what showed up in the World Series. Al was put into a position, and he responded to it.

Then when I led off the eighth with a double and came home on another double by Swoboda for a 4–3 lead, and Ronnie came home on an error for our final run of the year, it started to really hit me what a great team we were.

In our sweep of Atlanta in the NLCS, Al, Ron, and Donn had one at-bat between them, and now they had led us to World Series victory along with Agee and a few others. Everybody took part in our winning, and every day it was someone different. When we came to the ballpark, only Agee, Grote, Harrelson, and I knew we'd be in the lineup that day. And if your name was penciled in, those guys on the bench were always ready. It was a complete team effort, and whatever took place—whether it was the regulars or the guys platooning—something good was going to happen. It was amazing that our light hitters like Al and even Gary Gentry came through when they did. That Al batted .455

and Ronnie batted .400 and Donn won the Most Valuable Player Award of the World Series all circled back to Gil Hodges and how every one of us bought into his system.

There was some talk just a few years ago that when the ball that hit me caromed into our dugout, Gil took another ball and had another player rub it against his shoe. My opinion of Gil is that he never would ask one of our players to do something like that. Somebody else would have seen that. There's no way for me to know for sure because I wasn't in the dugout at the time, so I don't know for a fact, but Gil was not the kind of person who would try to win a game at any cost. I'll say this one more time, how could a ball bounce as far as it did if it didn't hit me? I know the ball hit me.

Gil Hodges wasn't just managing us, he was teaching us, and teaching us with integrity and honesty. I will never believe that Gil made a decision to doctor up that ball—he would never cheat like that, because he wasn't that type of person. He molded this team in his image and wouldn't tarnish what he'd preached by deceiving an umpire.

I haven't shared my thoughts on why and how I believe the 1952 World Series affected Gil Hodges into becoming a great leader. After another great regular season in 1952, Gil had one of those nightmare Series that guys have sometimes, going hitless (0-for-21) in the World Series against the Yankees. When you're as good a player as he was and everybody is suddenly getting you out, it's on you. When everybody is getting you out, and you're not having good at-bats, it's you, and you need to make the adjustment.

I think he learned a lot from that 0-for-21. I think he somehow embedded that in this team that if you continue to do certain things and you're not successful—it's you who needs to make the adjustment. And if you don't, you're the one continuing to suffer.

From that experience, I believe it told him you that you cannot keep making mistake after mistake and expect to be successful. You have to adjust and adjust often. If you're hitting really well and it gets around the league that you're hitting well and they know what you're hitting and what area of the plate you like, pitchers make the adjustment. Players talk. You have to know that, and you have to adjust what is going on, on a daily basis to maintain any kind of success.

I believe that 1952 World Series gave Gil a better understanding of adversity and how to overcome it. I believe that 1952 World Series gave Gil a better understanding of what it feels like to go through an agonizing slump and to then feel the pain of one of his players in the same boat. I believe Gil had that Series in the back of his mind when he was fortunate enough to play in four more World Series, where he more than made up for that 0-for-21 by batting close to .300 and hitting with power. I never heard Gil say any of this, but it's what I've always thought.

As for me, I may not have batted the way I wanted to in the World Series, but all that really mattered was that we won. I had the Mets first-ever World Series hit, scored the winning run in the final game, and made the final catch of the Series. What a lucky man—just some guy named Cleon from Africatown, Alabama.

Chapter 14

THE MOST DISAPPOINTING SEASON (1970)

I COULDN'T WAIT to get back home after the World Series was over to celebrate with my friends and family in Alabama, and therefore I missed the ticker-tape parade in New York and an appearance some of my teammates had on *The Ed Sullivan Show* where they sang a song from *Damn Yankees*. Looking back, I should have stayed in New York for the parade and gone home afterward. It was always on my mind after I watched my teammates being driven through the streets of New York in front of thousands of screaming fans throwing confetti.

But they had a big celebration for me and Tommie Agee in Mobile, where thousands came out to see us and hear us speak about our experience. Even Billy Williams had some words to say. For the three of us, we were always being approached when we came home. We were a close-knit community, and people were always rallying around us, sharing stories with us, and we were able to share our success with many of the young people. We always wanted to give back what we could, whether it was motivating them or just letting them know they had an opportunity to become major league ballplayers. There were a lot of kids like Norman Hill and Tank Brown who listened to us.

But winning the World Series brought all of that to another level. It highlighted the fact that not only are major league ballplayers from the Mobile area, but World Series champions are. Being native sons who just had won a World Series made us heroes to so many of those kids. We were the topic of conversation all over town. Everywhere we went, people were yelling and hollering and throwing kisses. It was special. We always had autograph seekers, people asking for mementos, taking photos. It was nice being someone so well respected, and I always gave back with my time.

We went to spring training the next year with a mission to repeat, and I thought we had an excellent chance of doing that. I thought we were building a dynasty with all our young arms and a real good farm system. We realized that we were a young team—an up-and-coming team with so much room to grow—and we thought most of us were going to get better as players. Our pitching staff was certainly going to get better with experience. The only thing that could stop us was ourselves.

Gil didn't have any meetings warning us or preparing us for any kind of letdown. That conversation never came up. We were certainly aware that other teams in the league would want to play their best against us—especially the Cubs—but Gil didn't seem too concerned about any of that. He just wanted to prepare us for the season.

I didn't set any performance goals for myself other than batting .300 or better, and that meant getting off to a good start and staying healthy. I realized from the 1968 season, when I ended up at .297, that I'd gotten off to a slow start, and when that happens it's hard to reach your goals. I concentrated on working hard during spring training and kept it in my mind to get off to a good start once we came north for the regular season. Being that the weather was usually cold in the first month of the season and I didn't like playing in cold weather, I knew that was going to be the toughest part for me. I loved playing in the hot weather, but the cold made it hard on some players to get the right timing down.

After my success in '69, there was no doubt in my mind I would have won the batting title had I not cracked those ribs. Before that happened, I was on fire and getting better each and every game, having good at-bats almost every time. That would have been nice to have won the batting title because it was a big deal back then. I knew if I stayed healthy I could challenge for it again.

When the 1969 season was over and I had a chance to think things over, I thought I should have won a Gold Glove, and everybody else thought so too. I was just trying to play baseball, so accolades and things of that nature weren't the most important thing to me, but what's fair is fair. I was the best left fielder in the league that particular year defensively (and offensively), led the majors in fielding percentage (.991), and made only two errors all season.

Before we went off to spring training, the great Johnny Murphy died in January. The Mets' general manager, Johnny Murphy was really the person we talked to and dealt with on just about everything. I remember a few times the Mets' chairman, M. Donald Grant, came into the clubhouse to give a little speech or pat on the back, but Johnny Murphy was our go-to guy. I remembered him most from the encouragement he gave me when he saw me my second year in Buffalo. He told me to stay strong and to never give up on myself, that I was a good player and would one day be a star for the Mets. That has stayed with me all these years.

Before we went to spring training, the Mets did some wheeling and dealing in the off-season that changed our World Series roster in a New York minute. Ed Charles was released about three weeks after the World Series ended, leaving us without a right-handed batter at third for Gil's platoon system. That was taken care of when we traded Bob Johnson and Amos Otis to Kansas City for their third baseman, Joe Foy.

Foy was a durable guy and a World Series veteran for the '67 Red Sox, but I think the Mets gave up too soon on Amos. We used to practice together back home, and I knew what he was capable of doing. But because he had no interest in shifting from the outfield to third base, he became expendable. I never saw it that way. Like all of us, he needed a chance to play, but our outfield was crowded with all those guys who'd proven themselves before. So the Royals gave him that chance.

He was a real talent, just in the wrong place at the wrong time. We always seemed to have a problem at third base—at least that's what the writers kept saying. And being that Amos was signed as a shortstop, the thinking was that he could handle third base. But after just a few games at third, Amos wasn't fond of the position and wanted to return to the outfield.

Look what Amos did the very year he was traded, playing every day where he belonged, in the outfield. In 1970, he played in 159 games with 620 at-bats, led the league in doubles (36), stole 33 bases, and made the first of four straight All-Star teams. He would end his career with more than 2,000 hits and 1,000 RBIs. Getting traded was probably the best thing that ever happened to him. But it wasn't the best thing for us and started a carousel of third basemen staying for a year or two and then gone. Foy showed little power and lasted just the one year with us.

Gone also were J.C. Martin and Jim Gosger, and during the season we sold Cal Koonce to Boston and Don Cardwell to Atlanta. When they raised our World Series banner at our home opener, we had some new pieces but were still a young team and felt pretty good about ourselves. I looked at our pitching staff and thought we had a dynasty in the making for years to come.

The Mets had one of the best minor league systems in baseball and introduced new players like Ken Singleton to support what we already had. We thought we'd only get better.

When we won on Opening Day in Pittsburgh, it was the first time in Mets history that that had happened. Eight straight years of opening the season with a loss had finally ended with that 5–3, 11-inning win, and the usual cast of characters picked right up where we'd left off in 1969. Tommie had three hits, Shamsky knocked in a run, Clendenon knocked in the winning runs in the 11th inning, Seaver went eight innings, and I got off to the start I was hoping for—going 2-for-4 with an RBI.

It really felt like 1969 again after that win, and there was no reason to think otherwise. I stayed hot for the first week or so, but we hadn't put together anything special yet, winning two, losing two, that sort of thing. But while we floundered around .500, the Cubs got off to a fast start by winning 10 straight games, and led us by four games in the standings. Of course, we knew they were out for blood after what happened in '69, and the Pirates were close behind them. That's when I went into the worst slump of my career, going from .407 in mid-April to .171 by mid-May.

I have no idea how I went so cold. I batted under .100 for an entire month with only eight hits, one home run, and a handful of RBIs. I had a sore wrist, but not enough to keep me out of the lineup. With me slumping, we were lucky the Cubs or the Cardinals or even the Pirates hadn't opened up a bigger lead, but the Cubs started losing after a hot start, and the Cardinals stayed around .500. We were only a half game off the lead when I started getting my stroke back.

I developed a mechanism for the purpose of not going into a deep slump by watching film after every ballgame to see if I was putting myself in the best position to get a good at-bat. I had learned so much about myself and about the game, I should have been able to do better than I did during that extended slump. Since we didn't have any batting coaches, we were usually left on our own to figure things out.

I finally realized that I was opening up too much and hitting a lot of hard ground balls at the shortstop, and many of those resulted in double plays. With my speed, I had no business hitting into to so many double plays, but I was hitting the ball hard and getting doubled up. That was a lesson learned when I hit into so many double plays, I knew there was something wrong.

Every time I'd hit into a double play, I'd go to the plate the next time thinking I was going to get a better result. There was no way I was going to come back to lead the league in batting at .171 in May, but I also never thought I'd end up leading the league in grounding into double plays with 26. Leaders in prior years were Clemente, Aaron, and Santo, but that gave me no consolation in the end.

In early April we went up against San Diego with a 6–6 record with Tom Seaver our scheduled starter. Seaver had pitched some memorable games for us already in his career, but I hadn't seen such dominance since his one-hitter against the Cubs in 1969.

We'd been in a record-breaking strikeout game before—when Swoboda took Steve Carlton deep twice to ruin his 19-strikeout performance—something Seaver would match this night. Even with only a few players putting the ball in play, we were very much in the game on defense.

What you have to understand is that, when Seaver or Koosman was pitching, they carried a rhythm when they got the ball, and they'd go right back to work. They never did a whole lot of waiting between pitches, and that put us in our own groove where we could focus on what he was doing. When you become uninterested in what's happening due to the lack of action on the field, that's when you make a bad play or get a bad jump on a ball. Guys like Seaver and Koosman worked fast and kept us in the game even when striking out 19.

There were some other high moments during that 1970 season, but nothing more satisfying than sweeping a five-game series in June with the Cubs in Chicago. We went into that series in second place, and when it was all over we were in first place, where we stayed for about a month.

The Cubs were certainly out for blood after that collapse in 1969, but after we left town they never recovered. I remember Agee and I were having fun with our home-boy Billy Williams, and Ernie Banks was chattering away saying, "This is our year. Last year was a fluke. Look at all those lucky wins. You'll never do it again." After that sweep, it sure didn't feel like he'd be right about them or right about us. Well, turns out he was wrong about the Cubs and right about us. The Cubs lost six more after that and never recovered, and the "luck" we'd experienced in 1969 was about to take a turn. But now we thought we were the team to beat and 1969 was happening again.

By September we stayed within a few games of Pittsburgh despite so many injuries to our starters. We still had a chance when we went to Pittsburgh for three games in September, and even with Seaver and Koosman on the mound, we got swept— 4–3, 4–3, and 2–1—the type of games we'd won in 1969. We went 6–9 down the stretch and fell to third place behind the rival Cubs.

Our record a year earlier in one-run games was 41–23, and this year it was 24–27. We were 6–12 against the Pirates and fell apart at the end. We weren't getting any timely hits, and the bullpen wasn't as strong as before. When they asked him about our season, Tommie Agee summed it up by saying, "The bullpen couldn't keep us in close games, and Cleon didn't hit early." I found nothing wrong with that because it was the truth. I kind of looked at myself as the spark. When your spark is not doing what he should be doing, then that puts a damper on things. I'll take that.

We thought we were on our way to being a dynasty, but because it happened so quickly and we were so young, we may not have been prepared for all the injuries and drop in production from players like myself. The 1969 season was the most satisfying year for a player, but 1970 was the most disappointing.

We were confident we'd bounce back from the disappointing ending to our 1970 season, but because of what happened and the rise of the Pittsburgh Pirates, the writers weren't giving us much of a chance, with many of them predicting another third-place finish for us, and I could see why. The Pirates had built a real strong lineup with Willie Stargell, Clemente, Dave Cash, Richie Hebner, Bob Robertson, and Al Oliver. They still didn't have a bona fide stopper, but they did have a bunch of 15-win-type seasoned veterans in their rotation.

None of that ever mattered to me, and they were usually wrong in the end, anyway. The baseball season is long, with injuries and trades, and you never know who might be having a bad year or a breakout year. It was important for a team's pitchers to stay healthy—especially for a team like ours that had been in so many close games.

It's hard to duplicate a season like 1969, and it certainly didn't happen in 1970. We weren't winning the same way we had been—especially not winning one-run ballgames at a clip that nobody could understand. The so-called "luck" we'd had so often wasn't there in '70, and naturally our opponents tried stacking their best pitchers against us.

Our lineup had hardly changed at all from 1970 to 1971, but we did lose Joe Foy over the winter in the Rule 5 Draft and brought in Bob Aspromonte to take his place at third. Agee was having a bad time with his knees most of the '71 season. Often I tried talking to him about not playing because he wasn't able to. He'd go off and get a shot and did the best he could do, but he just wasn't the same guy. In sports you don't mind people using you, but you can't let them use you up. You hurt the team and you hurt yourself. I'd tell him sometimes, "Just say you can't play today because you can't." He'd be up all night sometimes because his legs hurt so bad. He was in the lineup even when he was struggling, and he still had a tremendous year which shows you what kind of teammate and competitor he really was.

Other guys missed time from injuries, and that's what I'm saying. You don't plan for those kind of things. You hope when you leave spring training that the people you put on the field on Opening Day are going to be in the lineup the whole year, and that just didn't happen.

Just before the '71 season started, management traded fan-favorite Ron Swoboda to the expansion Montreal Expos for outfielder Don Hahn. When we picked up Hahn, I didn't know what the plans were for him or the future plans for the team because I didn't see him as an everyday player. Swoboda had the potential to be an everyday player because he had that natural home-run stroke and he was improving as a defensive player. I didn't see that trade as one that made us better, but a lot of things happen in baseball you don't understand. I didn't know the inner workings of that deal, and Gil Hodges didn't advertise what was on his mind or what he was doing. What he shared with you was what he wanted you to know, not what you wanted to know.

A lot of times when GMs go after players and don't get who they want, they end up with fill-in types of replacements, and that seems to me what happened from 1969 until 1972, when we got Willie Mays. We didn't think any of these guys we acquired were going to play every day in the starting lineup. We weren't picking up stars. In 1969 when we got Clendenon, we knew why we got him. He was going to strengthen the team against left-handed hitters. We all knew that. But when you go out and get the players we were getting now, it wasn't having the same impact, and it showed on the field.

Getting traded to Montreal was probably hard on Ron. When you go to another team and you're not a Willie Mays or somebody similar, you have to prove yourself all over again. I don't know if Ronnie had to do that or not, but I know he wasn't particularly happy about being traded—very few people are. And it didn't take long for the Expos to move Ron to the Yankees, just my point in why it is an organization goes after a certain player and moves him as quickly as they did with Ron.

You'd be surprised how often, when a trade is being worked on, you don't know until it happens that it's going to happen. Ronnie was a tremendous teammate, and I didn't want to see him leave, but that's baseball. I think all of us were kind of sad that he was leaving because he was good for the batting order. He was always in dialogue with somebody on the team about current events—both baseball and family matters. He was just a good teammate and a good person to be around. When you're a popular player like he was, nobody wants to see you move on to another team. Even though he wasn't an everyday player at the time, he was a product of the organization and a stabilizer of the organization. It wasn't a popular move with the Mets fans.

We were tied for first place briefly in June and only two games out by July 1. Then the injuries came, the Pirates got hot, and we started our free-fall in the standings, going just 9–19 for July and falling into fourth place—11 games behind. We never recovered after that, never even got close, and ended up 14 games back of the Pirates.

If 1970 was our most disappointing season, 1971 wasn't far behind. Koosman was hurt and won only six times; Nolan Ryan had blister problems again; but Tom Seaver and Tug McGraw both had stellar years. All in all, the pitching staff still led the league in team ERA (2.99), it just didn't feel like it to me.

For the first time in a while, I was healthy the entire year, and it showed in the numbers. I ended up hitting .319—good for sixth in the league—and led the team in all categories, even tied Tommie Agee in home runs with 14. There may have not been much more to say about the club, but baseball was making important strides for the Black man and for baseball in general, strides I'd been noticing for a while.

Emmett Ashford had already become the first Black umpire in 1966, and now, five years later, baseball had our first full-time Black broadcaster when the Yankees and WPIX named Bill White to the position. In February 1971, our home-boy, Satchel Paige, was selected to the Baseball Hall of Fame and was inducted in August at Cooperstown, becoming the first player from the old Negro Leagues to have such an honor bestowed upon him.

But even that was a bittersweet moment for most people of color. Certainly we were proud, but Satchel went into the newly formed "Negro Wing" of the Hall of Fame, not into the regular portion with all the others. To me, and maybe to others, that was like saying, "You can ride, but you have to go to the back of the bus."

In early September, the Pirates fielded an all-Black/Latino lineup for a game—the first time such a thing had happened in the majors. There was no big deal made about it when it happened, because the guys in the lineup didn't notice until the middle of the game.

All these things were significant to the Black man. You have to understand that by that time having a Black player on your roster wasn't just one or two guys like before, but several players, at times more than half the roster. The Pirates were loaded with

Black players, and we always seemed to have four or five with the Mets—far fewer than some other clubs. You could see around the league that Black players started dominating the scene, and when that happened, people's eyes opened up to the strength and roles Black people played in all sports. Look back to 1963 when Arthur Ashe became the first Black tennis player named to a Davis Cup team, that was significant to people of color. We'd come a long way in a short time, but there was a long way to go.

The same can be said when Curt Flood filed his lawsuit against Major League Baseball and Commissioner Bowie Kuhn. Curt didn't want to go to Philadelphia in a trade and refused to go, and who could blame him? Philadelphia was rough. They didn't like anybody. They didn't even like their own players. We all paid careful attention to that. When Marvin Miller got involved, the reserve clause became a good thing for all sports. It gave us more control and a respectable retirement system, the right to negotiate and to fight back like Curt Flood did. Before all that, we were just playing, having fun, and not realizing how much money was being made by ownership and how much of that was being given back to the athletes.

Most of us would have played the game for nothing, but it didn't seem fair any longer. Our pension situation wasn't great, and hardly anything could be done about it because we didn't have a voice. When you signed with a club, you became their property and could do only what they said to do. When Marvin Miller came in, all those things changed, because he made us realize all of that. It was like being enslaved because you didn't have a say in your future. He visited every clubhouse in the spring and emphasized to all of us that we needed to be treated like human beings, not like property, and that we were going to be part of the change.

Chapter 15

GIL, JACKIE, AND ROBERTO (1972)

THERE WAS A PLAYERS' strike during spring training in 1972, the first one ever in the history of the game. It lasted about two weeks but resulted in more pension money and salary arbitration for the players. It also took away some games from the regular season that resulted in an uneven schedule from team to team.

On the second day of the strike, our season—and our lives—changed for the worse. Gil Hodges was out playing golf with our coaches, Joe Pignatano, Eddie Yost, and Rube Walker, when he collapsed while walking to his hotel room. The heart attack he suffered was fatal.

At such times it was difficult to process something like that. We'd been focused on the labor strike and keeping up on its progress and hoping the season would start on time, staying as sharp as we could during the waiting period. The news was devastating and almost hard to believe. Gil was like a father figure—like Superman to us—and never did we have any inkling that the minor heart attack he suffered in '71 was that serious. He was still a young man, so alive, and appeared to be healthy. But through the heartbreak we all felt, there was still baseball to play.

We opened at home against Pittsburgh with Seaver and McGraw combining for a five-hit shutout under terrible weather conditions. It wasn't baseball weather, but it was April weather—cold and blustery in the 40s, not fun to play in.

We'd been used to seeing large crowds on Opening Day, but it seemed empty to me (15,893). We all wore black armbands in memory of Gil and would continue to do so for the rest of the season. They played taps, we watched a video about him, and the Mets announced they'd retire his No. 14 jersey.

Most of us thought Gil's death would bring us together emotionally, that it would serve as something we'd think about during the year and keep alive at all times. To a man, we all wanted to dedicate the season to Gil, to bounce back from what happened the last two years, and to win it all for him. The first order of business, of course, was to select a new manager, and the Mets wasted no time promoting Yogi Berra to be our manager, a choice I was disappointed in. I wanted Whitey Herzog, our farm director.

Whitey was not only a good baseball man, but he knew everybody because he had worked throughout the organization. Whitey was a hands-on baseball man who taught and believed in the fundamentals of the game and was the closest person we had to the way Gil ran things. Everybody on that ballclub had some interaction with Whitey because he was in the farm system, and I think not only myself but most of us wanted Whitey to be our next manager. I still wonder even today why he wasn't chosen. All those people who came after Gil, they were good baseball men, but Whitey had an edge. I just don't see why the organization didn't see that.

I didn't see Whitey as a manager per se, but as an instructor, someone who taught baseball. I saw him as someone fundamentally sound and who was approachable and knew everybody in the organization. Those are the kinds of people you need to manage because they know what's in the organization from top to bottom and how to interact with both management and players. To me, he had an edge on everybody. I was very disappointed.

It's always the case in New York to go with a known name like Yogi. I'm not saying Whitey was an unknown quantity, but if you're running an organization and you lose someone like Gil, how do you go about replacing him? Name recognition? You've got to throw that out the window. You've got to think about how to bring all those ingredients together, like making a cake. The ingredients you put in that cake determine how that cake comes out in the end. Whitey certainly was a known quantity in our organization, and all the players liked him. I just didn't get it. The Mets missed another opportunity to keep someone like him in the organization. He knew all the guys in the big leagues—even the guys we had traded for. And not only that, he was so sound in the fine points of baseball.

But you never know what the relationships are between the front office and the personnel. Maybe no one saw him as a manager, or maybe they didn't think he had managerial skills or what have you. But if you knew him, if you talked to him and were around him, it stood out. He was a great baseball man and a great baseball mind, and look at what he became after he left us.

After Yogi was named manager, he had a meeting with the team. Yogi was a great player. He was good for baseball because of who he was, whom he'd played for, what he did in the game, and what he brought to the game every day because of his personality and demeanor. All of those things were great, but they didn't equate to being a great manager.

We were happy the coaching staff stayed intact. Rube Walker was the bench coach and the pitching coach, and Joe Pignatano was more like the enforcer—at least he was when Gil was managing. Joe carried out commands and relayed Gil's thoughts to the players about different things, whether it was being late or being in the clubhouse when you should be on the field, or doing things you weren't supposed to be doing. During the season, you're supposed to be on the field at a certain time, and naturally every now and then somebody's going to be late or whatnot. Pignatano would write you up, and there might be a fine.

Eddie Yost was the quiet one, but he was a good teacher and had good baseball instincts. Everybody liked him and rallied around him because he always had a smile and a good relationship with everybody on the team. I'm not saying the others didn't have it, but we named him "Good Kid" because he was such a good person.

The coaching staff was a well-oiled machine. Everybody had a responsibility and was in sync. Gil assembled a great group, and we all rallied around one another and liked one another. I'm not saying it was different in that regard with Yogi, but when a new manager comes in, it isn't the same atmosphere. It wasn't the same belief and skill set from Gil to Yogi.

With Shamsky and Swoboda both gone, we needed a right fielder and acquired Rusty Staub from Montreal just three days after Gil died in exchange for Ken Singleton—another one of those young guys we let go too soon. Don't get me wrong—Rusty was a good player and a good teammate—but Kenny had already shown some power for us, was only 24 years old, and was a switch-hitter who didn't need to platoon. We had no switch-hitters, and having one or two guys on your roster who can switch-hit can change the way an opposing manager makes his pitching moves. I was sorry to see him go. And like Amos Otis, Kenny had over 2,000 hits for a career and made three All-Star teams. Rusty had some good years with the Mets, but his better years came before he arrived and after he left, making All-Star teams the year before he got to New York and the year after he left.

Of course, you can't play hindsight in baseball—or in anything for that matter—and you go into a trade hoping to get something better in the deal, not knowing what lies ahead. Rusty was a good player and he was popular, so the deal was a decent one at the time for both sides. With Rusty in right, Tommie in center, and me in left, there was no room for young John Milner—an outfielder/first baseman with some pop in his bat.

So Yogi moved me over to first base in May and June, and I ended up playing more at first than in the outfield. I played plenty of first base in high school and in Sunday and weekend ball, so I wasn't a stranger to the position, I just hadn't played it since being in professional baseball. John Milner was an up-and-coming player who played both first base and the outfield. It looked better in some people's minds that I go to first base to take Kranepool's spot because I was playing better at that time than he was, rather than directly exchange Milner for Kranepool. I never asked, but that was my take on it. Why would you bring me in to play first base when Milner is a first baseman and an outfielder? I just think they were doing something so the press wouldn't get into it. Kranepool to me was a good talent. He was a good, steady first baseman. Maybe he wasn't hitting well at the time, but we all knew they were just trying to find a way to get Milner into the game. I was in the game either way, and it wasn't about two lefties being in the game together, or righty-lefty matchups. I was fine with it, but I felt better in left field because that's who I was, I was an outfielder. I had good enough hands and could play the position.

It would have made more sense to put Milner at first instead of Kranepool, but how would the press have handled that? In New York, it's all about that, what the press was going to say or react to, and how that might create a news cycle, a problem for management. I remember one time I pinch-hit for Kranepool—a lefty-righty situation—and some writers had something to say about it. There was a "How could I pinch-hit for Kranepool?" sort of a racial dialogue, as I recall. That existed. Who's better in left field—Jones? Pete Rose? Lou Brock? Nobody was better than I was defensively in left field for the Mets. That's my point. They should have put Milner at first base.

None of that would have bothered Gil. He would have paid no mind to any of the noise going around from the press. He would have done what was right for the team and not be worried or influenced by all that.

We acquired Willie Mays in the middle of May, and that move marked the end for Agee, though he didn't know it at the time. Willie was 41, and like most players that age, his production wasn't what it once was. He'd been under .200 for the Giants and hadn't hit one home run, but with the Giants having a rising star in Bobby Bonds and the Mets trying to bring Willie home, the deal was made.

We weren't sure how Yogi was going to use Willie, but like most aging superstars like Mickey Mantle and Ernie Banks, he started to play some at first base, and that's where Yogi put him in his first game with us—incredibly against the Giants at Shea. Tommie and myself were happy to be back at our regular positions in the outfield and hoped this new logjam of players would take care of itself.

Like a script from a movie, Willie hit a home run in the game, a game that was played on Mother's Day before a crowd of more than 35,000. When he got back to the dugout, we greeted him with big smiles and congratulations. That had to be quite a moment for Willie in his glorious career. He'd played in five World Series, was named MVP twice, had been an All-Star every year since 1954, and had already hit more than 640 home runs.

That game would become our third win during an 11-game winning streak that stretched our half-game lead to six over the second-place Pirates. Our new pitchers Ray Sadecki, Danny Frisella, and Buzz Capra were pitching well, along with the usual from Seaver and Koosman. I was hurt for a while during that stretch, and Milner filled in nicely. Rusty was hitting well, Tommie was still playing center, and Willie was playing part-time Then all our good fortune came apart with a string of injuries that took what was once a strong lineup into an average one, and by July 1, the Pirates caught up to us in the standings.

It was a carousel of guys getting hurt and going on the disabled list. Jerry Grote missed over half the year with bone chips in his elbow. Rusty fractured his wrist when he got hit by a pitch in July. Buddy broke his wrist a month later against the Reds. I missed more than 50 games with an assortment of injuries, and Tommie was nursing a sore knee all season long. Add to that off-years for Gentry and Koosman, and it made it hard for a team to get into a rhythm with key guys in and out of the lineup like that.

Because of those injuries, we struggled with some of our replacement guys. They were all good players and good teammates, and they contributed to some wins. But they weren't the front-line type, and by August 1, we'd fallen six games behind, continued to lose, and finished 13½ games behind the Pirates.

Injuries are part of any team's season, but the number we had and the games people missed were out of the ordinary. By season's end we didn't even have one player with 500 plate appearances. Not one of us managed 100 hits or 20 home runs. We were dead last in the league in stolen bases, and despite all our firepower, I led the team with only 52 RBIs. Considering all the injuries, some people were surprised we'd finished with as good a record as we did. But after a 25–7 start, we played below-.500 ball.

Even though it was one of those years, we witnessed some of the good things baseball gives us every year—like the day in June when Willie and Hank Aaron were on opposing lineups in the same game, both of them tied for second-place on the all-time home run list with 648.

I had a great interest in the history of the game that I was taught about on the fields of Africatown. I'd learned about the greats of the game by all those elders telling their stories—stories that fascinated me and helped draw me to the game, helping me imagine what it felt like being a major league ballplayer. Of course, Hank was a home-boy and struck up a relationship with me. I'd played against Willie a few years before the Mets traded for him and remembered listening to the World Series on the radio when he played for the New York Giants. Now he was my teammate, and his locker was next to mine.

I didn't play that day, but I was in awe of both of them and felt humbled and blessed to know and talk with them. It was highly unlikely that something like this would ever happen again, where two of the greats from our generation faced each other on the same day tied with so many home runs. Neither one hit a homer that day, but it was pretty special to see them on the same field.

We were in Pittsburgh at the end of September. The Pirates had already clinched the division, and the great Roberto Clemente was looking for his 3,000th career hit. I wasn't in the lineup again. Clemente wasn't a power hitter like Mays or Aaron, but he had won four batting titles, was a perennial All-Star, and even at the age of 37 was hitting well over .300. Roberto lined a sharp double down the left-field line in the fourth inning, and we saw history being made again. He joined Willie and Hank and a handful of others to reach that milestone.

I remember thinking at the time how difficult it must be to get all of those hits, and for Willie and Hank to get all those home runs. I'd only reached about 900 hits with more than 2,000 to go if I ever was to hit that mark. That put it into perspective for me, that I really was watching one of the greats of the game.

It was a dark day for baseball on the last day of 1972 when Roberto's plane went down while delivering supplies to Nicaragua. He was only 38. I heard about the plane crash the next day, and it was like losing a brother. It was a great loss for the game of baseball and humanity—especially knowing how his fellow Puerto Ricans felt about him. He was a treasure, and he did it the way nobody else could. Some say he did everything wrong at the plate but he had great results behind it. You wouldn't teach hitting the way he hit, but it was right for him.

What he did was in him like it was in with me. He was a man of stature, and it was his calling. Some people are called to preach, some people are called to teach, and some people are called to serve. He was called to serve, and he served his entire island. I believe everything is predestined, and we just have to act out what's already on the wall of your life. He'd probably always been aware of the need to do something more for others than for himself. He looked around and saw a need and acted on it. I'm certain he looked at who he was and what he accomplished and how he could take being famous into being a blessing for others. I've said this many times before, that those who depend on you are seeking a hand up and not a handout.

I didn't think about it then, but I think about it now, how good the Almighty was to wait to call Roberto home after he got his 3,000th hit—a milestone hit that put him next to the greats of the game.

It was only a few months earlier that Jackie Robinson had passed away at age 53. I can't begin to describe the impact Jackie Robinson has had on my life in all I do and all I say. I know this, that Jackie Robinson set the table for players of color and took the hard road like a Superman, and that he is with me in spirit throughout my life and into today.

Our 1972 season was perhaps the most difficult season for us to endure both on and off the field. We lost Gil Hodges, Jackie Robinson, and Roberto Clemente. Before the season started, we had vowed to win it for Gil. It was disappointing, to say the least. I was looking forward to coming home for the winter.

Chapter 16

"YA GOTTA BELIEVE" (1973)

WE FELT LIKE we were competitive in 1973, but I didn't think we had a world championship team when we left spring training. We had fielded competitive teams since 1969 but never came close to becoming the dynasty we all thought we'd be. And now other teams in the league had gotten better and passed us by. The Pirates had won our division for the past three seasons, winning it easily in 1971 and 1972. The injuries had really hurt us, which was something we hoped wouldn't happen again. It had been a year since Gil died, and we all missed him and his leadership. It wasn't the same without him. We didn't talk about it much, but it was in the back of our minds that we wanted to still win a World Series for Gil.

I realized I was having good seasons every other year, and 1973 landed on a good year. It wasn't something I could explain, other than some nagging injuries and cold April weather, but as it is with all players, I wanted to get off to a fast start and get back to hitting .300.

I went 3-for-3 on Opening Day against the Phillies, hitting two home runs and driving in all our runs off of Steve Carlton—the same Steve Carlton Ron Swoboda had hit two home runs off of back in 1969 when Carlton broke the strikeout record. I'm sure when I went around the bases after hitting my second home run, it reminded Carlton of that day. But I didn't keep my good start going, and after going 0-for-7 in a doubleheader at Chicago, I was down in the .240s, hadn't homered since Opening Day, and suffered a leg injury that ended up nagging me all season.

It was the last thing I wanted after missing a third of the 1972 season, but I was hurt. And after being out for about a week, the rumors started going around that I wasn't dedicated and showed lack of effort at times. Some folks started to blame Gil Hodges for the way he handled me when he came out to get me in the outfield in the Houston game in 1969, that I never got over that and appeared uninterested in playing hard, that I wasn't hurt as bad as I said I was, and all that.

But I've said it before and I'll say it again—I had nothing but respect for the man, and faking an injury was no way to honor him. I wanted to be out on that field with my teammates, contributing and playing hard, but I was hurt and couldn't run or pivot the way I needed to. We ended April tied for first, but I wasn't ready to come back and missed the entire month of June. I didn't finally feel right until early July. Getting your stroke back after missing all that time could be difficult, and I still hadn't homered since Opening Day. It took me a handful of games before I felt comfortable, and from July 7 to the end of the season, I was in the lineup every day. But I never put together any hot streaks or any slumps until mid-September, when we made our move in one of the most unusual seasons imaginable.

We'd already sold Jim Fregosi to Texas in July, a move that everybody could see coming. He was a great teammate and a good person to have on your team, but he never really won his position because his production was nothing like what he'd done with the Angels or what we'd expected from him. He was supposed to be the guy at third base everybody wanted, had been an All-Star for the Angels, and was someone we'd traded Nolan Ryan and three prospects for. But he'd had a down year before we got him, and his struggles continued with us. He struggled through all of 1972, and it got worse before he was sold to Texas, where he suddenly started doing better.

I don't known if it was playing in New York that caused such a drop-off in production, but never did I want them to trade Nolan Ryan for anybody. We'd already peddled away Amos Otis and Ken Singleton, and now in a span of less than two years we had no Nolan Ryan or the guy he was traded for. You can't just give away talent like that and expect to win.

By early July we'd dropped to 34–46 were in last place, 12½ games behind the first-place Cubs. There was half a season to go, but not only were we so far behind, we had to climb over four other teams in our division just to get within striking range of the top. At such times you're thinking about doing things in stages, like passing one team and then the next and getting to .500. That's easier said than done.

It looked like the Cubs were finally going to get that division title that always seemed to slip away from them late in the season. They always seemed to falter the last two months with all the hot weather and the day games in Chicago. But they were hot now, held a five-game lead over the Cardinals. Like us, and without Roberto Clemente, the favored Pirates hadn't gotten it going. The standings almost looked upside down with us and the Pirates at the bottom of the division. Even Montreal and Philadelphia were ahead of us in the standings.

We'd just been swept by the Braves at home when it felt like we'd hit rock-bottom, because that's where we were—especially after the second game of our three-game set against Atlanta. We trailed 6–3 going into our half of the eighth. I'd gone into left an inning earlier for George Theodore after the speedy Ralph Garr hit an inside-the-park home run that got by him. We hadn't been coming back from any three-run deficits late in the game, but we took the lead after eight when I walked, came home on a two-run single by Willie Mays, and took the lead on a two-run double from Garrett.

We had Tug on the mound for the ninth, but he hadn't been right all year. Just a few days earlier in Montreal, the Expos knocked Tug around pretty good, along with the rest of them that day. We lost that game 19–8, and Tug gave up seven runs in about an inning of work that inflated his ERA to over 6.00—not a number any team can win with. And it wasn't only in that particular game that he struggled. There'd been plenty of games he was giving up walks, hits, and home runs while recording just an out or two. There was plenty of blame to go around for where our record was, so you can't just blame Tug for where we were. All I knew was we needed him to figure it out and for us to figure it out if we were to have a chance.

But it wasn't going to be this night. Tug gave up three more hits in the ninth, and the Braves scored three times to win the game. That was really our season in a nutshell to that point. Those were game we'd always won before, games you needed to win in order to compete in the division. When a season is over, you look back on games like that one that you know you should have won.

But Tug was such a free spirit and didn't let it bother him much. Most guys would be visibly upset, and some guys would throw a cooler or punch a wall, but Tug was Tug and took it all in stride. He was calm when he should have been angry, but that calming and lovable manner of his was infectious. There was no one better to root for than Tug McGraw.

Tug was an interesting character. He was a great teammate and would slap his glove against his leg a few times almost every time he walked out to the mound as a reliever. People in the stands probably didn't notice, but we all knew, and when we saw that we knew he was fired up and ready to pitch. He was a character. We did a lot of things together, and whatever came up came out. He didn't care who was around and how they accepted it. We might be out having fun, and he'd jump up and say something funny to get everybody going. He was comical—a great teammate and a winner. He was a loose guy at all times.

But Tug cared about his performance and went to see a motivational speaker the day of our next game against Houston. Tug handled failure his own way, so we weren't surprised when he started going around the locker room telling us what the speaker had said to him, that "you've got to believe, you've got to believe." Of course, some of us laughed a little and smiled about it, but we could see he was serious and that he was internalizing those words and believing them himself. It's funny sometimes how timing can be, or whatever else you want to call it, because M. Donald Grant had decided earlier that day it was time for a locker room pep talk.

I wasn't much for pep talks, but this was a good one. Mr. Grant told us we could do it, that we were a good team and there was still time left to make our move. He reminded us about the 1951 Giants, who overcame a 13-game deficit late in the season to overtake the Dodgers, and that we could do the same thing, and that we should "believe in ourselves."

Now this was right after Tug had gone around the locker room saying the same thing, so when he heard Mr. Grant utter those words, he blurted out, "Believe! Ya gotta believe!" like some street preacher standing on a soap box. Tug danced and moved around the clubhouse, repeating the phrase, but we could tell by the look on Mr. Grant's face that he found no humor in it and thought Tug was mocking him. I think Ed Kranepool went out to explain the situation to Mr. Grant, and when they came back into the locker room, Tug hadn't stopped talking or moving around and kept repeating, "Ya gotta believe." That night we beat Houston 2–1, and when we got back inside, Tug was reminding us that we gotta believe.

They say timing is everything, and certainly that was the case with this. Had Tug gone to see his friend a day or two later, or had Mr. Grant decided to address the team a day or two earlier, none of this "Ya Gotta Believe" stuff would have happened. It seemed like more than just a coincidence, two events coming together at just the right time.

But all the words and all the rallying cries didn't seem to help after that. We lost four of seven before rallying for a win with a seven-run ninth against the Braves in Atlanta. Then we won a few and lost a few and remained in last place into early August. The Pirates and Cardinals had overtaken the Cubs a while back and were tied for first, with barely winning records. The Cubs had gone into a huge tailspin during that time and were only a game ahead of us in the standings. As hard as it was to believe, we still had a chance.

We did have a decent August, our first winning month since April, but I wasn't doing as much as I wanted to, to help the team. My batting average stayed around .260, where it had been most of the year, but I wasn't producing runs. By mid-September I'd homered just once in two months and hadn't driven in a run in well over a week of games. We split two with the Cubs, and I knocked in a few, but we still trailed going into Pittsburgh, though only 2½ games behind them.

It was odd knowing what the standings were in our division. It had become a real logjam—only Philadelphia had fallen out of the race, and the Cubs were playing the way they usually do in the last two months. We were three games below .500, in fourth place in the division, and like the other teams around us, we hadn't put together a decent winning streak. We all knew that if any of the four teams got hot right now, the division could be won.

The talk in Montreal was real, and they'd been comparing the Expos to the Mets—both expansion teams that finished last or next to last every year then suddenly surprised everyone like we did in '69. They'd won six in a row twice already in September, sweeping the Phillies, the Cubs, the Cardinals, and the Phillies again, and looked like they could be that team that got hot at just the right time. But in between those two streaks, we took three of four from them in Montreal. They didn't have a lineup or a pitching staff that struck fear into you like the Pirates or the Cardinals, but our old friend Kenny Singleton had become their best player and was doing a lot of damage. Right after that, however, they lost seven straight games and fell out of contention.

I don't know that we felt like there was a chance for us to win it until the last two weeks of the season. We had injury after injury to our keys players. I called Grote our Hall of Fame catcher because he was the best I ever saw at the position, and Buddy Harrelson was the best defensive shortstop I ever played with. Both guys were missing months of the season, and Willie Mays had such a swollen knee he couldn't do a lot of things Willie could do before. When he was able to play, he was as good as ever, but that wasn't very often.

On September 16, we were 73–76, 2½ games back of Pittsburgh, and set to play the Pirates the next five games—two at their place and three at Shea. We knew we had to take at least four of five to hope to have a chance. The Pirates were a dangerous club and had been the dominant team in our division since 1969, winning three division titles and the World Series in 1971. They didn't have a stopper like Seaver or Koosman, but they had Willie Stargell, who was good for 40 homers and well over 100 RBIs, and solid players like Richie Hebner, Al Oliver, and Dave

Cash. What they didn't have—sadly—was Roberto Clemente out in right field.

The Pirates certainly had Roberto on their minds, as we did after Gil died. It's traumatic for a team to deal with something like that, and as the season wore on, it was natural to think about that sometimes. We thought about Roberto when we were playing the Pirates and looked out to right field and someone else was there. At such times, we would think about Gil Hodges and the big hole in our hearts because of that. Pittsburgh was playing for themselves, but they were playing for Roberto, too. We were playing for ourselves and for Yogi, but we were still playing for Gil. You want to do something special to honor somebody's memory. Things like that are always in the back of your mind, especially when it's right in front of you.

But in the first game, they got to Seaver early and never let up. Our 10–3 loss put us 3½ games back but five back in the loss column. It wasn't hard to do the math. With only 12 games to play, we had to win the next four against them. It didn't look good in the second game after eight innings, when we trailed 4–1. If there was ever a time to say, "Ya gotta believe," this was that time. Another loss wouldn't eliminate us, but it would come close to that. Six games out in the loss column with 11 to play and two teams ahead of us was a hard task. But like 1969 all over again, we rose to the occasion.

After Buddy flied out to start the inning, our next seven batters reached base, and we scored five times to give us a two-run lead. Pittsburgh's rally fell short in their half of the ninth, and instead of being 4½ back, it was 2½. That was quite a trip home, and Tug started in on his, "Ya Gotta Believe" routine. And he was right. We'd fought all the way back from where we were early on and had a chance to go into first place coming home with three against the Pirates.

I finally felt like I was getting my stroke back in the first game at Shea when I homered off Nelson Briles to give us the early lead, then homered again in the eighth to put the game away. It was the first time I'd hit two homers in a game since Opening Day and the first time I'd driven in five in over two years. Of course, I was happy to contribute like that when we really needed it—the Pirates' lead over over us had been cut to just 1½ games, and now we had a chance to take the lead with two more games in New York.

The atmosphere around Shea Stadium felt much the same as it had in 1969—electrified. Every player wants to be in a pennant race this late in the season, and every player wants to have something to do with a win. The fact that I had five RBIs the night before motivated me even more to do what I could do to help the team again.

Tug had really turned his season around since he started to "Believe." He had one bad outing in August, then allowed just one earned run in his last 22 innings of work in September, with seven saves and three wins. You can look at a season any number of ways, and there's no doubt we wouldn't have been right on the heels of the Pirates without a September like he had.

In Game 2 the Pirates scored first on a fielder's choice in the fourth, and we tied it 1–1 on my two-out single in the sixth that drove in Felix Millan. Dave Cash knocked in a run in the seventh to make it 2–1, and Millan tied it at 2–2 in the bottom of the inning with an RBI single. Cash doubled in another run in the ninth to make it 3–2, and the Pirates were celebrating as if they'd already won.

It felt right that we'd come back from two deficits in the game, but we headed to the ninth needing another run to tie and two to win. They brought in righty Bob Johnson to face Grote, but Yogi countered and sent Ken Boswell to the plate to pinch-hit.

It was another of those risky moves by Yogi, but he was playing the percentages, and we needed a base runner. Grote had proven to be a good clutch hitter, and if we tied the game and sent it into extra innings, Ron Hodges would have to take his place behind the plate. Hodges was a good player, but there was nobody like Jerry Grote. Ron had done a good job throwing out runners but hadn't played much under those kind of pressure situations.

Boswell had been used mostly as a pinch-hitter since mid-August and came through a few times with some hits. But he was having an off-year, batting in the low .200s most of the year. We needed him to come through like he had in 1969.

Boswell got perhaps his most important hit of the year when he singled to right to start the inning. He moved to second on a sacrifice bunt from Don Hahn, then scored on a pinch-hit, two-run double by Duffy Dyer, tying the game at 3–3 and sending the fans into a frenzy.

It was another unlikely hero at the time because Duffy had been in a season-long slump. He got it together somewhat in August but hadn't even reached .190 at any point of the season and hadn't knocked in a run in two months. Getting two huge hits from two struggling guys certainly was an unlikely occurrence, but you see things in the game sometimes that don't add up, that you may have never seen before.

The game did go into extra innings, and Ray Sadecki came in for us in the 10th, setting down the Pirates in order. Then, after we couldn't score, struck out the side in the 11th, and set them down in order again in the 12th. We had runners on base in both the 11th and 12th, but couldn't score. In the 13th, the Pirates' Richie Zisk finally broke through against Sadecki with a single and stood at first base with Dave Augustine batting with two outs. That's when one of the craziest plays I've ever seen or was a part of changed our season for good.

I knew when Augustine hit it, it was going behind me, either off the wall or over it, so I got into position to play the carom. The way it hit the top of the wall in that precise point made it kick back rather than go over the wall, and that surprised me because I had never played a ball off the wall in that manner before. When the ball hit off the top of the wall, it went airborne, so I positioned myself to get it back to the infield as quickly as possible. It was the perfect bounce for me to get under and make the relay. The thing that was so exciting about it was I was able to play the ball off the wall as if the wall itself was relaying the ball to me. You don't practice taking the ball off the wall in flight. It was a one-of-a-kind thing that happened. I made a good throw to Wayne Garrett at shortstop, and he made his relay to Ron Hodges, who had come in for Jerry Grote at catcher. Hodges blocked the plate and tagged Zisk out easily.

You practice relay plays all the time, but you don't practice for a ball coming off the wall the way it did. Usually a ball that hit off the wall would bounce off the ground, and as you picked it up, you'd turn to find your relay man. I had to watch the ball all the way to my glove to make sure I had it, and when I turned I saw Wayne at the edge of the infield. I made a pretty good throw to him and he made a perfect throw to home.

Had that ball bounded away to the left or to the right, I had put myself in a good position for that, but Zisk probably would have scored. That made the difference in the game—we might not have won without that play. The place went wild, people were up on their feet clapping, just so ecstatic over what had just taken place. Not only do you hardly ever see a play like that, but it happened at a crucial juncture of the game. It had to have taken something out of the Pirates, but we were energized by that play. When Ron Hodges singled in Ken Boswell to win it in the bottom of the inning, we mobbed both of them.

There was an air about the place that hadn't been there for a while—a feeling that we thought would be there ever since our 1969 season. It felt good, and it felt right again to have played— and won—another "miracle" game.

There was little time to revel in what had happened just 24 hours earlier, but everyone was talking about that "off-the-wall play," and it was shown on all the TV stations for quite a while after that. That's the beautiful thing about baseball—there's always a game tomorrow when you can either forget about what you did the day before or hope to continue something special, where the intangible of momentum either stops or continues.

We'd pulled to within a half game of the Pirates, but still had two more losses than they had. At this point of the season, that all-important loss column was being looked at closely, and although we'd gotten close, it was the Pirates, not us, who really controlled their own future. Even if we beat them this one last time, they could win the rest of their games, and there'd be nothing we could about it.

Of course, that would require a season-ending, 11-game winning streak for them, and that seemed unlikely to happen, but not impossible. They had a seven-game winning streak earlier in the year, so they had it in them to go even further, and one thing you never do in a baseball season is discount anything from happening—case in point being the previous day's game.

It wasn't just the Pirates to be concerned with, it was the Cardinals and the Expos—both with records like ours that clogged the standings and made things entirely too interesting. Before our miracle victory over the Pirates, we'd been in fourth place behind all three of them, but the Expos' loss to the Cubs and the Cardinals' loss to the Phillies turned things around—at least for a day.

The standings were so close, people were talking about—and many hoping for—a four-way tie at the end of the season. They'd been comparing our race to the American League pennant race in 1967—before division play—when so many teams had a chance up until the last day of the season. Then the Tigers split a doubleheader with the Angels, and the Red Sox beat the Twins to win the pennant. The only difference was those teams had winning records, and there was a chance the top team in our division might not have one.

It seemed likely it would come down to head-to-head matches, and all of us had games to play against each other. You can't look ahead, but our homestand was ending with one last game against the Pirates and then two each with the Cardinals and the Expos. The Pirates and Expos still had seven to play against each other, and the Cardinals had us, the Cubs, and the Phillies. This would be survival of the fittest. We had to keep winning.

It was about a month earlier when Yogi and I had a conversation at my locker. Sometimes he called me "Jonesey," and sometimes he called me "Slim." He said, "Slim, we could win this thing, we still have a chance. But if we were to win it, you'd have to lead the guys, because they believe in you. I believe in you." I told him I was as healthy as I'd been all year, and if it took everything I had in me to do what he was asking, he'd have that from me. He smiled, went back to his office, and from that point on kept reminding me of what he said.

As a ballplayer, you always want to produce, but when the manager singles you out like that—especially at this time of the year—it gets inside of you and motivates you even more. It had been only three years, but I had memories of that 1970 season and how I let the team down with my slow start, and it had been four years since the 1969 glory year when I was injured toward the end. That's the other beautiful thing about baseball, you can put that all behind you, but it's always in the back of your mind. You can't change any of it, but you can remember.

I'd been out most of the year but was healthy and swinging a good bat. My two home runs the day before the "ball off the wall" game kept me in a good groove I'd been feeling for about a week. It wasn't that I was getting a lot of hits, but I was driving the ball with authority.

We beat the Pirates that day behind Seaver, then swept two from the Cardinals, and split with the Expos, our loss to them ending our seven-game winning streak. By then we'd moved into first place, but the Pirates were on our heels and tied with us in the loss column. The Expos had nearly been eliminated, and the Cardinals were hanging on by a thread.

The home runs continued down the stretch for me. One each against the Cardinals and Expos, then two more against the Cubs that gave me six in the final 10 games. Along with 14 runs batted in, I was contributing like I knew I could, and needed to.

There were certain situations during my career when I went to the plate thinking about hitting a home run, but during that stretch I was reminiscing about '69 and how I was in control. I was healthy again, in control of my thoughts and my approach so that, when when I got my pitch, I didn't miss it. Each time I went to the plate during that period, I thought about my conversation with Yogi and about '69. I knew I was going to drive the ball somewhere because that's how good I was feeling at the plate. It didn't matter who was pitching. That's what it was all about. Not thinking home run, not thinking about driving the ball, just focusing on having a good at-bat every time I went to the plate.

There'd be no four-way tie or even a two-way tie. We beat the Cubs in the first game of a scheduled doubleheader on the last day of the season in Chicago to clinch it. It was raining hard enough for them to call off the second game well before it started. I remember celebrating with Willie Mays and feeling great because he would have a chance to go to the playoffs and possibly the World Series. I felt good about that for him, and we felt that we could beat anybody at that time. The division was ours. Our 82–79 record was the worst ever for a first-place team, but none of us looked at all that—we were looking at the Cincinnati Reds.

It felt much the same as it did when we played the Braves four years ago in the playoffs—the Reds had a potent offense with guys who could hit the ball out of the park. Their top three home-run hitters had nearly as many as our entire team. Tony Perez hit 27, Joe Morgan had 26, and Johnny Bench hit 25. Add in Pete Rose and Bobby Tolan, and we knew we had our work cut out for us. They'd won 99 games in the regular season, but unlike Baltimore in 1969, they had to struggle.

They went into early September tied with the Dodgers, thanks to a seven-game winning streak from late August to early September and another one after two losses. Their 14–2 record coupled with the Dodgers losing nine straight put them in the driver's seat, where they stayed comfortably after that.

Our record against them was 4–8, but most of those losses were early on, with all four of those wins coming in July and August. Like I've always said, none of that mattered and wouldn't now. It was nice being the underdog because the pressure was all on them.

The Reds took Game 1 in Cincinnati, when they rallied for runs in the eighth and ninth to win it—a home run from Rose to tie it and another from Bench to win it. We managed only three hits off of Jack Billingham—including one from Seaver, who had our lone RBI—before he gave way to the bullpen in the ninth. Our biggest chance was in the first inning, when I grounded into an inning-ending double play with the based loaded.

Game 2 was almost a repeat of Game 1, with us leading 1–0 after eight innings. But we broke things open with four runs in the top of the ninth on singles by me, Grote, and Harrelson. Then Jon Matlack shut them down in the ninth. We came home and took a 2–1 series lead with a big game from our offense and another stellar performance from Koosman. Four of us—myself, Don Hahn, Rusty Staub, and even Koosman—had two hits each in that 9–2 win. We had a chance to clinch the pennant the next day, but the offense went cold again, and we lost in 12 innings on another Pete Rose home run that tied the series.

We'd managed just three hits in a game for the second time in the series and gave up key home runs to Pete Rose twice. Both home runs Pete hit reminded me of the Orioles' Don Buford when he did it against Seaver in Game 1 of the '69 World Series— both unlikely guys in their lineup to go deep. We'd kept their real power hitters in check, but like he'd done so many times before in this career, Pete "rose" to the occasion.

It all came down to Game 5 at Shea, and we took an early lead when Kranepool singled home Felix Millan and me in the first inning off of Billingham. They tied it in the fifth at 2–2, but we scored four runs in the bottom of the inning when I doubled with Wayne Garrett and Millan on, scoring Garrett. Millan then scored after a John Milner walk and a Mays single. I was forced at home on a grounder to second, but then Milner scored on a fielder's choice, and Mays came home on a Harrelson single. We tacked on one more in the sixth and coasted from there. We had won the National League pennant again.

Before the start of the 1973 World Series, it was the first time I'd ever felt scared about something. I was afraid that we weren't healthy enough to represent the National League. I told this to my wife at dinner in Oakland before the first game, and she was surprised at that. I told her I wasn't afraid for me, that I was afraid we wouldn't be able to represent the National League because of all the ailments and injuries we had on the ballclub. Felix Millan was hurt. Rusty Staub was hurt. Mays was playing on bad knees. She said I'd be all right, and I knew I would be. It was the rest of the team I was concerned about.

When All-Star Games were played, we were serious about them because we were the better league and wanted to show that. The only All-Star Game the NL lost during my time was in 1971. We dominated that game almost every year and were proud to do so. Same thing when it came to the World Series. After the Yankees dynasty ended, the National League put together a pretty good showing. Not like the All-Star Game, but from 1963 to 1969 we'd won five of seven. We wanted to show the world that we belonged there and could win it.

My fears were calmed down after we tied the Series with a wild extra-inning affair in Game 2—a game that featured 28 hits, six errors, 11 pitchers, and any number of crazy plays. It took over four hours to complete, but we scored four times in the 12th on two errors and a clutch single by Willie Mays.

Earlier in the game, Willie had had some bad moments, tripping at second base and missing a fly ball in center. I'm sure he was embarrassed, but what people don't understand about Willie misplaying that ball in center field was that he had a bad knee. His knee was all swollen, and he was put in the lineup and played. He could have said no, but like the trooper he was, he went out there. His knee gave way on that play, and it may have looked bad, but all of his teammates knew why it looked bad. Three weeks prior to that, his knees weren't as swollen, but now they were. We talked as players and teammates all the time, but I knew the situation because his locker was right next to mine and I could see that his knee was swollen. When his knees were healthy, he was like the Willie Mays of 1955, doing the same things in the outfield with grace and ease just like he'd done all his career. He made only one outfield error that whole 1973 season, and if he had played a whole season, he might have won another Gold Glove.

There were some days he shouldn't have played, but who was better on that team than him playing on one leg? I had the pleasure in being in the same outfield, locker mates, and talking to him each and every day just sharing baseball stories and everything else. It was one of the highlights of my career.

I was right there in position and could have made the play, but he was Willie Mays, and he made plays like that all throughout his career with ease. I sure wasn't thinking about calling Willie Mays off the play.

I think about him every day because he turned 90 in May 2021. A lot of the little things he could do people might not think about. For example, if he was on first and the catcher blocked a pitch in the dirt and it rolled 10 feet away, Willie Mays would be standing on second base. He was just so good at every phase of the game. Nobody really recognized his ability to steal bases and take extra bases and take advantage of every possible situation he could. In his prime, he led the league four times in stolen bases and probably would have had a lot more 50-homer seasons had he played at a place like Shea Stadium instead of Candlestick Park.

But in the '73 World Series, Willie was hurt and could hardly lift his leg. I don't know if he ever let on about it, but it was true.

We could have won that Series, but Yogi was influenced by the media. He didn't take any chances. After winning Game 2, we dropped Game 3 in extra innings in New York but came back to take Games 4 and 5, with a chance to clinch it back in Oakland. If I'd been manager in Game 6 against Oakland, I would have pitched George Stone, then you would have had Seaver on one more day's rest and Matlack, if needed, for Game 7. If you really want to break it down as to why we were able to win our division, look at George Stone. He pitched well and won five games in September for us, but Yogi hardly used him in the World Series. He was an unsung hero for us.

But everything was about the press in New York. Why do you think George Stone didn't start in the World Series when we were up 3–2 against Oakland? It was all about the press. I don't know if it was Yogi's preference or if he was influenced by someone, but he ultimately made the decision to start Seaver. Whitey Herzog wouldn't have been worried about the press. Whitey would have been managing. Managers like Gil Hodges, Casey Stengel, and Ralph Houk never would have listened to the press or worried about it.

Losing that Series in seven games gnawed at me for a while. We had them three games to two and let it slip away. Perhaps there'd be another chance at a ring somewhere down the line, but after '69, I'd seen how hard it was to get there.

Chapter 17

THE CYCLES OF LIFE (1974)

AS WE APPROACHED the 1974 season, all eyes were on Hank Aaron and had been since the end of 1973, when he came within one home run of tying Babe Ruth's all-time home-run record.

There are records in baseball most of us never thought would be broken. Joe DiMaggio's 56-game hitting streak, Ty Cobb's 4,191 hits, Babe Ruth's 60–home run season, and of course the biggest of all—Ruth's career total of 714 home runs. We'd already seen Roger Maris hit 61 home runs in 1961, so anything was possible now. I'd always been fascinated with all those records and wasn't one who thought they couldn't be broken, because in my mind, records are meant to be broken and would be one day.

But Hank had already reached the age when most ballplayers had retired when he made his move. He was 37 years of age in 1971 when he hit a career-high 47 home runs, then hit 34 more in '72, and 40 more in '73. When the season opened in '74, he was 40. On April 8, 1974, Hank passed Babe Ruth, hitting his 715th career homer at home off of Al Downing into the Braves bullpen. Of course, we were all proud of that incredible accomplishment—especially all the home-boys like Hank's brother Tommie, Tommie Agee, Willie McCovey, Billy Williams, Amos Otis, and me. It was a record-breaking feat of mammoth proportions, and it had been done by a Black man.

The off-season of 1973 brought us all back to Jackie Robinson. Hank had received death threats like Jackie had, but he was strong. And unlike Jackie, he had us—other Black ballplayers to talk to and to receive support from. It reminded us all that we'd come far and made some strides, but there was a long way to go to fixing all that—especially in the South.

I met Jackie just before his death in 1972 and had a conversation with him. I told him how my grandmother and my great-grandmother loved him. He used to come up to the ballpark quite often, though rarely into the clubhouse unless he went up to Gil's office. He would come and sit in the dugout, and I got the chance to talk to him. He was bigger than life to me.

I was in awe when I spoke to Jackie and always wanted to keep telling him how much I—*we*—appreciated what he went through, and that he delivered for all of us. When you've got the entire Black race standing on your shoulders each and every time you go to the plate or take the field, that kind of pressure is real, and not everyone could've responded to it as he did. He was able to do that. It was enough to be on a ballclub when you were always on the road, so to speak. You might ride with the team on the bus, but you couldn't go to the same hotel. You might ride with the team on the train but you couldn't eat where they ate. You couldn't do anything, so it was hard to create a team concept when you were on an island all by yourself. You had some people on the team like Pee Wee Reese and Eddie Stanky, and probably Gil Hodges and Duke Snider, who treated you like a brother, but there's no way you felt like a brother when so many are yelling "nigger" at you.

Before all that occurred, there were quite a number of trades and player movements made before the start of the season at the winter meetings in Houston that included some big-name players. Willie McCovey was traded by the Giants to the Padres;

Jimmy Wynn went to the Dodgers; Willie Davis went from the Dodgers to the Expos; Felipe Alou was put on waivers and claimed by the Yankees; and even the great Juan Marichal was no longer a Giant—sold to the Boston Red Sox for who knows what.

It was hard to imagine the Giants without McCovey and Marichal. I'd watched them both back in 1963 when I first came up and could hardly believe 11 years had passed since that day. Thinking about that reminded me of the day my teammate, Frank Thomas, told me how fast a career goes by and to appreciate every minute of it. Frank was 34 years old at the time, was in his 13th season, and on the decline.

He'd had a super year in 1962—almost matching what he did with the Pirates in '58 when he had 35 home runs and 109 RBIs, but he was broken down some by '63, and his production wasn't even close to what it was the year before. After the Mets traded Frank to Philadelphia in 1964, he went from team to team, hoping to find a home and to rediscover what he once had. When the Cubs released him during the 1966 season, that was it.

Our battles with those old Cubs teams were over—at least against the guys we played against, which started with Ernie Banks's release a few years earlier—the end of an era for baseball. Ernie was to me the best shortstop in baseball ever, at the top of my list, considering his defensive and offensive prowess. To me, Ernie Banks wasn't just Mr. Cub, he was baseball's ambassador. Ernie's best years were behind him, though, and it was time.

It was also time for all those other Cubs players we played against to move on, and it seemed to happen all at once. In the winter meetings, the Cubs traded away Fergie Jenkins, Glenn Beckert, and Randy Hundley. By Opening Day they had moved Ron Santo and Jim Hickman—even Leo Durocher was gone. All they really had left from that 1969 squad was Billy Williams and Don Kessinger, and Billy would be next, a year later.

Your rivalry with a team is predicated on several factors, and our rivalry with the Cubs was full of them that started in 1969. But when you take away almost all of the key players, that rivalry undergoes a change—maybe not to the fans, but certainly to the players who'd been there. We battled those core players for five years both on the field and in the standings, and now a new core of players like Steve Swisher, Andre Thornton, Bill Madlock, Rick Monday, and Jose Cardenal had taken their spots.

I wondered if Billy Williams or Don Kessinger felt the same way about us, because gone were Tommie Agee, Donn Clendenon, Ron Swoboda, Nolan Ryan, Jim McAndrew, Ed Charles, J.C. Martin, Cal Koonce, Don Cardwell, Al Weis, Ron Taylor, and Amos Otis, replaced by guys like Rusty Staub, Felix Millan, Don Hahn, and John Milner.

All that gets you thinking about all your old teammates, your special rivalries with other clubs and players, being traded, getting old, retiring—all of it. You think when you're young that slowing down and producing less won't happen to you, but it does. It always will because Father Time is in charge of all that.

We didn't make the player moves so many other teams made in the off-season to strengthen themselves, or move all our aging players like the Cubs had done, and because of that and other reasons that 1974 season was a polar opposite of what both the Cubs and the Mets had been experiencing. We didn't battle for first place or even make it interesting. We fell into fifth place in April, dropped to the bottom of the division in June, stayed there until late July, and finished the season in fifth place—five games ahead of the Cubs.

We were still a fairly young ballclub, but all the injuries we had been experiencing kept coming back. Grote and Buddy both missed about 60 games. Seaver started having trouble with his back, which showed in his ERA and won-lost record. He got treatments between starts but was never himself all year. I started to have problems with my knee at the end of '73 and in '74 I missed around 40 games. My injuries seemed to compound themselves, and I tried to compensate for it.

I didn't remember injuring my knee in a game and started looking back at my football days. Then I remembered when I got hurt. It came from an injury when I was a freshman—I stretched some ligaments and damaged some cartilage. That injury kept me out the whole season. After that year was over, my knee seemed to be at 100 percent, until it started bothering me years later. I had been a running back for five years, carried the ball 30 or more times every game, handled the kickoffs and the punt returns, and played every down on defense. I was on the field for the first play of every game and for the last. I hardly ever came out of the game.

I didn't realize at the time that all that punishment would show itself in later years, that it affected my body after taking all those licks and hits. I realized later that there had been nothing in baseball that had caused my knee to start hurting, that it all stemmed from football. At the time I thought if I stayed in good shape, I could pay no mind to it. I was the star player on the team and wanted to be out there because I knew my team needed me and I enjoyed it. I never talked to anybody about this when I first started having problems with my knee. Despite my knee giving me problems, I got off to a good start with my average, but we started out 3–11 and weren't putting very many men on base. I don't remember many times coming to bat with men in scoring position, and I had only five RBIs by late April.

I don't recall any panic that took place when we started out 3–11, but I did sense that our lineup wasn't quite as potent as it had been the three previous years. Don Hahn wasn't the player they hoped for, but he was in a tough spot replacing Willie Mays.

He was great kid, a great teammate, and a super defensive out-fielder, but I never saw him as an everyday center fielder. That's who we had, though. And although Rusty Staub and John Milner were doing a good job for us, all the replacement guys going in for us during all those injuries weren't producing. When we put that lineup together, they would more often kill a rally than sustain one.

If you look at all the close games we lost, you know why we had a bad season. I started learning about all that and paying close attention in the off-season to such things, and when I saw what our record was in one-run games (17–36), I wasn't surprised at all by it because we walked off the field as losers so often.

The dynasty we thought we once had never materialized. We'd gone from a team that won 100 games to a team that lost 91. It felt more like the '68 Mets or even before that, and for the first time in years it showed itself at the gate.

We'd gotten used to big crowds since that 1969 season and led every team in attendance from '69 to '72. Our peak year was the year after winning the '69 World Series, when we averaged more than 33,000 per home game. But the numbers were sliding: 28,000 per game in 1971; 26,000 in '72; 23,000 in '73; and 21,000 in '74.

Our final three home games of that 1974 season against the Phillies drew about 5,500 per game, and it felt like being back at the Polo Grounds again, a far cry from the 50,000 fans we'd played in front of in Septembers past. By that time the Mets had brought up Benny Ayala in August from Tidewater, and he started playing a lot in left field. I knew what he was going through, and he did all right—much better than I did in 1963 and '65, when I first had my chance on the big-league roster.

It made me think about the cycle in baseball, and how every player experiences it at one point or another. It had already been more than 10 years since I was in Benny Ayala's shoes, when I was that 20-year-old looking for a spot on a major league roster and trying hard to make an impression. I could understand everything he was feeling and shook my head that I was no longer that guy, that I was more like Frank Thomas and other guys back on that '63 club—an elder statesman and no longer a rookie.

We shared Shea Stadium with the Yankees that year and the following year while Yankee Stadium was undergoing a renovation. Our paths seldom crossed because of the way they had to schedule our games, but I got to know Lou Piniella and Bobby Murcer during those seasons. Murcer would talk about the old Yankees teams that dominated for decades, and how even that had ended.

It reminded me of the Cubs dismantling their entire team in the spring, of all the guys gone from our '69 team. Just a few years after the 1964 World Series, the Yankees started losing all those players that had them playing ball in October. By 1969 almost all the Yankees everyday starters were gone—Tony Kubek and Bobby Richardson had retired; then they moved Elston Howard, Clete Boyer, Tom Tresh, and Roger Maris to other teams.

I never dwelled on such things, they just came to mind as I saw things happening, things changing. I was still only 31 years old and had seen it all, the good times and the bad. I knew we had a tough road ahead of us in getting better, but like the Cubs, the Yankees, and now us, I was right there inside those changes, part of the ebb and flow of a baseball career. And while I hadn't been traded, I could better understand what Warren Spahn, Ken Boyer, Tommie Davis, and Ralph Terry might have been feeling.

Chapter 18

THE VAN (1975)

WE BROKE CAMP in spring training 1975, and they decided that I needed to go back to Florida to get better, rehab, and to be in a better situation where they could work on my knee every day. The plan was for me to go to the ballpark every day, get treatment, and workout. I thought I'd be there for a week or two, stretching my knee and getting ready to get back on the field and play every day.

After a workout one day, I had some friends who asked me to go fishing with them the next day. I had a rented van, so I could drive over to where they were. I planned to first go by the hotel near the place where one of the guys lived and pick him up to go with us. I went to a club on the beach the night before and some of the other younger guys were there with some other people I knew. I also knew one of the waitresses—Sharon Ann Sabol—and she asked me if I was going back to St. Pete if I give her a ride home.

I just wanted to do something nice for someone, and it seemed innocent enough to me to be a nice guy, and so I said I would. We hung around the restaurant for a while, and when her shift was over, we got in the van together and headed for St. Pete. We shared the usual small-talk on the way. I told her I was going fishing with some friends, and she said she liked to fish and wanted to come with us. I told her it wasn't my boat and couldn't say yes or no, but she could ask the guy once I got to his place. But before that, I had to go by the hotel to pick up some things.

There were no cellphones then, so we got back in the van and started over to where my friends said they'd be playing cards and would save me a spot. We drove on and kept talking, and I never noticed the gas gauge indicated the tank was almost empty, and before you know it, we ran out of gas.

This was very early in the morning, when everything was closed, but I felt safe that we'd run out of gas on a busy street with a service station nearby. I said I wasn't sure what we should do. There was no reason for us to get out of the van and walk somewhere because everything around us was closed. I never liked to hitchhike and thought it wouldn't look good or be our safest option, so that's when we decided to sit there and wait for the service station to open.

Of course, I was upset with myself for not checking the gas gauge and was sure my friends would start to worry—especially since they knew where I was staying and that we had already left the hotel. The only thing left for us to do was to try and get as comfortable as we could, so I stayed in the driver's seat with her in the passenger seat, and before long she said she was cold.

I took off my jacket and gave it to her to keep warm. She wrapped it around her and went into the back of the van. A few seconds later, I saw the red flashing light behind me. The cop got out of the car and slowly walked toward me. I rolled down the window, and he asked me what was wrong, and I told him we ran out of gas. He said he didn't see anybody else, and I told her there was a young lady in the back of the van. He went and opened the back, and that's when all hell broke loose.

I hadn't yet said whether she was White or Black, and when he saw that she was White, he asked again what was wrong with a whole different tone to his voice. I don't know if he called for backup or they just happened to show up, because right then another car showed up and other officers got out to check out what was going on. They talked it over for a minute, and that's when the first officer said they were going to arrest both of us. Well, that surprised all of us—even the other officers asked what we were being arrested for. He announced was he was going to arrest her because he found marijuana in her purse, and he was going to arrest me for indecent exposure.

I hadn't seen any marijuana, and she certainly didn't smoke it in front of me or even ask me if she could. I was fully clothed and had only given her my coat to keep warm. None of what he was saying was true, but I knew I was in a bad spot dealing with a bad cop. He must have had some vendetta with me being Black and her being White, because he didn't give me another chance to defend myself. But he handcuffed her while the other officers tried to talk him out of it, to talk some sense into him, that they believed I'd just just ran out of gas and he should let us go. He sounded like the big man in charge of a big case and announced it was his case and ignored everything the others were telling him. They took me down to the station and pulled the van, but they never did arrest me.

The next morning all I heard was that I was naked in a van, having sex with a young White girl. Naked! In a van! Never happened then, never would happen in the future. I'm a grown man. I've done a lot of things before I was married, but I wasn't naked in that van. That was a lie—a hurtful lie that would never go away no matter how long or how hard I maintained it as gospel truth. Then when it went out all over the wire services, I knew there'd be more defending myself to my family, and probably the Mets would be involved. It was just a matter of time before the hammer came down and came down hard.

By now, M. Donald Grant had called the hotel, wanting to get their version of what they knew. All they could tell him was that they saw me leave with a young lady, but that was all they knew. They saw me come into the hotel to pick up some things and said I stayed just a minute or two.

I wondered how the story got out like it did, and I found out later that the cop who made such a big deal out of nothing got fired over something else, I don't know what. He never told the truth even later, but the other cops who were there knew what the truth was and that I wasn't lying. I can only assume it was that one cop who called the wire services and told them his made-up story.

I had to come back to New York to explain my story to Mr. Grant, but it was no story. Mama Myrt had instilled in me at a very young age that the truth will set you free, but I never really understood what all that meant back then. I just knew to tell the truth at all times—even when you knew you'd get in trouble for whatever it was you'd done. So I'd never had anything to do with being dishonest or deceitful, and this van incident was no different.

Mr. Grant met with me and wanted me to face the press to apologize, and I agreed. I had no problem being up front with people in a situation that I created, and the only thing I was guilty of was being in the wrong place at the wrong time with no real motive or knowing I was doing anything wrong.

At some point you have to face your demons and realize that you put yourself in a situation. Whatever I had to do by explaining it to the public was necessary for me to go through. There was no crime, and there was no nakedness. They said I was found naked, asleep in a van with a young lady, that I was under the steering wheel in the driver's seat. That when the police light came on, I rolled the window down and got out of the van to explain to him why we were there. Who would walk out of a van naked?

All I knew was I had to get through those interviews. The only thing I was worried about was my wife and what it was doing to her and my family. In order to set things straight, I had to tell my side of the story over this bald-faced lie. I don't recall if she heard it first on the news or if I told her first. I called her, and we talked about it. She was upset, but I told her the truth of what happened. She said I needed to come home. She was in New York with my babies. It was a hard pill for me to swallow because of what I had done to them. She believed me like she always had.

That episode—parading me in front of all those reporters—did not sour my relationship with Mr. Grant because he did his research and found out that what I'd told him was the truth, and he accepted that. He asked me how I felt about apologizing to the media for the situation I was in, and I told him I would. I felt bad about the situation, but I didn't feel bad because I had done nothing wrong. I was with a young lady, but not for the purpose so many people thought I was. There was nothing going on sexually. The plan to go fishing with my friends was the truth. I didn't understand how something like that got out into the public or what I would have to go through to make others happy.

I had to move on, but it was something I never left behind me. Whatever feelings or thoughts the people had about it at that particular time, they were likely to maintain. Some people want to believe the worst about people. They want bad things to happen and for somebody to talk all about. I don't care how much you try to explain, they see the situation and feel like anything else is bullshit. Bad news sells, and it always has and always will. I was at ease about it because I knew it didn't happen. The truth did set me free, and I wouldn't succumb to bullshit. I didn't ignore the press or stop talking to them after that, even though

I was already leery about them because they don't always print what you say, but what they want you to say.

I knew it was in people's minds once I got back on the field. I was somewhat conscious of the fact that it hurt my career and it hurt my credibility. I'm aware of that. My saving grace is that I know what was said was a lie. That's why I'm at peace with it. But it hurt.

Nobody said anything to me about it, be it a teammate or an opposing player. In fact, I never discussed it with anybody once I made my statement about it being a lie, and my teammates treated me like they always had and had my back.

Being a Black man prepares you for situations like this. You're scrutinized and sometimes you're put in situations that if you were White would never happen. I come from the South, so I'm aware of who we are and what the world is like and how a certain segment of the population is treated. You live and you let live, and you try not to put everybody in the same bucket. Everybody White is not a demon and not a hater, and crises come up that I see taking place now that I've seen all my life. You wonder why a man would want to hurt another man for bullshit. To some people situations like this just added to the scars of their lives, but to me they are rallying cries. They are motivators. They are things that make you see and do things that have a way of lifting you up in these situations.

I read these words to the media that day: "I wish to apologize to my wife and children, the Mets' ownership and management, my teammates, to all Mets fans and to baseball in general...I am ashamed...I am basically a good man and have no desire to be bad."

When it all ended, Mr. Grant said, "I hope he will not be persecuted here by anyone." But it was the beginning of the end of my Mets career. Going back to that van incident and with everything still happening today in the Black community, it gets you to really wondering how far we've come as a nation and how far we need to go.

We look around us today and see what's happened. There are a lot of things the White population takes for granted. And we talk about our rights to do certain things, but it's not a right for all people. And suddenly this country is a great country and it could be even greater if we just went back to Jim Crow and to the White mandate to do one thing—suppress the Black folk.

We were there just to serve, and many in charge of us had no sympathy or empathy, or even understood that we had feelings and families and desires that they simply took away. At any time someone could be minding their own business, just going on with daily life, and an angry mob could decide to hang them. Or they decide to go to the jailhouse and break somebody out because he allegedly did something, then hang them with no consequences because the law enforcement turned a blind eye to the whole thing.

When you think of all those things, it is sometimes difficult. How do you talk to your kids about those things? They should have the same opportunities, the same ability to pursue happiness, to be the best they can be, as any other man. But when there's so much pulling you down, it is hard. The only way these things can change is if we can continue to fight as Black folks and Brown folks, but the White population will only be changed by the White population. There won't be enough change until they decide to talk among each other and decide that this world is better off if we can all push in the same direction rather than pulling in several different directions.

We've had George Floyd situations since the 1800s and especially since 1865. When we were enslaved, we had no rights. They took away our dignity, and we just did what we were told to do.

There were one or two who always decided that they wanted to be free, but for the most part we as Blacks just tried to survive and didn't fight for equal justice because we were too busy fighting for our lives.

There's an exhibit in Montgomery, Alabama, that depicts what happened from the 1800s up into the 1940s about lynchings. You can't imagine how many people were hanged for no reason at all. The sad part about it is mobs came and cheered and watched the lynchings as if they were sporting events. When I talk to my White counterparts, I express myself in a way that I want them to see me, that I'm a man—not just a Black man, but the way I see them as men. Not as White men but as men. What's in your heart and what's on your mind? How can you and I make the world a better place?

I have these kinds of conversations with my ex-teammate Ron Swoboda more than anybody else. We've become close friends, and he's the kind of guy who will say what's on his mind, not say what you want to hear. I'm proud to have him as a friend because I like that about him, but we need more people like him who understand. We're fighting all of these demons, and the same people who are supposed to be serving mankind are the same people who are killing us.

The George Floyd situation is different in some ways. Yes, it brings to the forefront all the things that have happened down through the years, but it all changed because one young lady had the foresight to film what she was seeing, and stay there filming until the end. And so George Floyd was killed over a counterfeit $20 bill? We can say why that was happening, but it's not the reason. If he had passed a counterfeit bill, why would he have stayed around talking? He would have passed it and left. But no, they wanted to show their dominance just like they had during the slave days. I don't know. Maybe if George Floyd had been 5'2" and weighed 120 pounds, this guy wouldn't have exploited the situation the way he did. But George was a big guy, and the cop needed to show who was in charge and so he went too far. Why are you arresting a guy for a counterfeit $20 bill when you're not even sure he did it? Why couldn't you have given him a ticket and make sure he showed up in court and let the court deal with him? Why were you the judge, jury, and executioner? There have been many situations like this over the years, but they weren't caught on video. The world isn't going to change overnight because of this, but it's going to be a better place because of this young lady who filmed the action.

We can learn from history that this may not change a lot of folks' minds, especially those who were raised to hate. It's a cruel world, and we've accepted it—and when I say *we*, I mean people in general. If we hadn't, then we would have done something about it years ago.

Why did all this hate come about all of a sudden after the abolishment of slavery and the end of the Civil War? They controlled the Black man and the Brown man and the Yellow man and the Red man and still weren't satisfied. But as soon as we fought for our rights, the anger intensified and the haters kept it up. It's hard to take, knowing this still exists in some places, that the attitude that people of color don't deserve the same freedoms and rights as White people still goes on.

Take the removal of the Confederate flags and statues of Confederate generals, for example. It's a good thing because it makes a statement that this is not who we are. And who celebrates losing? The South lost the Civil War, but they celebrate it every year. Why? Because it's something they think they need to hang on to and is part of who they are. But it's none of those things.

History tells us all the time that what goes around comes around. A certain part of the population doesn't agree with the removal of statues. The sad part about it is, a part of the population that doesn't agree doesn't really know much about it. How can all these hate groups exist? Where do they come from? What part of the population—north, south, east, or west? What makes someone a hater? Why, because you need someone to hate? Or did something happen to you or your family that caused these kind of ideals that brought you to the point where you are?

Most of the haters can't answer that question. They need something to hate, somebody to hate. I go to bed every night with the idea of having something good to do the next day. That's my plan. These haters go to bed every night conjuring up who they can hate, why they hate, and how to show it. We get back to equal justice. The playing field is never going to be level, because there's too many people who'd rather be hating and stepping on people than picking them up off the ground. There's too much of that hate, not enough love and kindness.

But none of this deters me from being the one who can make a difference to others—even when another racial incident happened to me again just two years later in 1977. We owned a restaurant in Mobile called Cleon's, and we had a friend who owned another restaurant in the same neighborhood. It was good food, good times, and we got to see a lot of our friends when they came out.

We were getting ready to close one night. I was going to meet up with the other owner, and Angela was going home for the kids. I drove over to the other restaurant and sat down and talked to him for about an hour, then drove back to our restaurant and saw a cop car behind me. I hadn't thought much about it because I hadn't done anything wrong, but in the back of my mind I couldn't help thinking about the van incident from two years before.

So I turned into our parking lot and starting to get out of the car to go back into my establishment, when the cop pulled in behind me. I got out of the car and asked him what seemed to be the problem, and he said my turn signal wasn't working. I thought he was just letting me know about it, so I thanked him for pointing that out. That's when he asked for my driver's license and registration, and I knew I had them in my other car.

I was back in my car at this point, so I asked him if I could go inside to call my wife to bring over the documents. He said that would be fine but wanted me to remain in the car until he said so. This was still long before cellphones, so there was no way to get hold of Angela. I must have sat there for 15 minutes or so. I finally got out of the car and asked him what was going on, was he going to let me call home or give me a ticket? At that point, two other police cars pulled into the lot. I said, "What's going on here?" The first cop walked up to me and said they were going to whip my black ass.

They didn't recognize me, and I said, "What did you say?" and a few of them replied, "We're gonna whip your black ass, nigger." I said, "You mean you're gonna fight, because I'm not just gonna stand here if you start whupping my ass." So he drew back his stick, and I took him by the arm and put a grip on him so hard he couldn't raise it up. But the other two were coming at me, so I ran for my life.

I should have stayed on the street, but I headed for the main highway instead. Something told me to run that way, but when I jumped across a fence, a dog was on the other side, coming at me. So I jumped back over the fence where one of the other cops was waiting for me. He went to hit me, but I flipped him over. Then I got hit in the head with a billy club from one of the other officers. By that time, all the neighbors had rushed out of their houses to see what all the commotion was about.

They started yelling, "Is that you, Cleon? What's going on?"

I said, "These guys were trying to beat me up over nothing."

Lucky for me, two Black officers arrived who recognized me and put a stop to it.

A lot of conversation went on, and I don't remember going down to the station. A judge I knew got involved, and whatever charges they'd drummed up on me, he got them to drop. Later on that story got into *Jet* magazine, and it upset a lot of folks.

That makes it hard to trust the police when they target you for a small thing like a broken turn signal—especially in the South, where some of them still are fighting some kind of war inside. I know plenty of White cops I can call friends, and I'm not saying all policeman are bad, but when a cop goes on his shift for the sole purpose of harming and harassing Black folks, you find yourself always looking over your shoulder, always ready to run or protect yourself. Those cops were no different than the cop I faced in Florida, bad guys with agendas and ulterior motives.

With all that happened, it took me back to all the others who'd fled for their lives but had no one to help them. It gave me an idea of what it must have been like back in the days of slavery to be on the run.

Chapter 19

YOGI (1975)

I HAD SURGERY on my knee during the winter of 1974 when the team went to Japan for a barnstorming tour. I stayed back to have knee surgery, which I should have had during the middle of the season. I knew my knee was really in bad shape even then, but they thought we had a chance to win—but not if I wasn't in the lineup.

Of course, I wanted to make the trip to Japan with my team-mates. I wanted to meet the people and understand the Japanese culture and compete against the best Japanese players. We knew there'd be big crowds for the games, and it was really a big deal for them.

I wanted to come to spring training early to get treatment each and every day before the regulars came to camp. To that point, the Mets didn't give me any special instructions or any rehab program, so I was just on my own trying to figure out what was best for me during the healing process. I was working out, but I started to develop problems with other parts of my leg—my calf area and the tendons along my ankle didn't acclimate as they should have. I told the Mets all this and they still denied me.

By the time I arrived at spring training, I wasn't having problems with my knee, I was having problems with my calf and ankle, and my Achilles tendon had turned black. In fact, I could stick a pin in my lower leg, and it was so hard I couldn't feel a thing. Once the trainers saw that, they worked on it some, and I came around a little bit, just not enough to start playing.

That's when I started to get fed up with baseball and was in a bad way. I didn't want to do anything because I was sick. I was injured. I'd had surgery and was practically on my own. I had tried working out and went to see the doctor a few times before coming home to Mobile. Everything I did I did on my own, and had put in calls to the front office and was denied. Even to this day, I don't know why. I asked the Mets' general manager, Joe McDonald, if I could go to spring training early because I was having those lower leg issues and needed some help with the rehab. He said they weren't letting anyone go to spring training early. They denied me that, but they said yes to Joe Torre, who went to early camp. My thing was Joe Torre was just coming over in a trade, and I can understand his wanting to get acclimated with his new team. I understand decisions and how people need every opportunity to adjust to a new organization to see how they fit in. I had no problem with that.

I thought that was really small of them. I should have been in early camp because I just had surgery, plus, I was a veteran player on the team who should have been shown a bit more respect. The way the situation was handled, some adjustment should have been made. No one had seen me or talked to me about how my knee was coming. I thought it was coming along well. When you've never had surgery you don't know what to expect and when to expect it, but I knew I was having a problem when I ran. I was lifting weights and walking, but I wasn't working every area of my leg like I should have been. That became a problem. My leg was never 100 percent after that.

My rehab took a while, and I missed about 40 regular season games before I was able to play. I hit a pinch-hit single and drove in a run in my first game back, then started out in left field the next day and batted third like I always had. A few games later I went 3-for-3, and everything seemed to be going just fine.

During my absence, the Mets had used slugger Dave Kingman and John Milner mostly as my left-field replacements. I didn't really have a relationship with Dave Kingman. I knew him from the Giants and as a player and a teammate I didn't heave any real interactions with Dave.

He was a teammate, and I wished him well. It didn't matter that he was in left field or whatever, because I felt if I was healthy, he wouldn't be in left. He'd be in another position, and I'd be out there. He could hit home runs, but I was more valuable to the team in left field because I could do everything. John was one of the players I tutored, and he was a pretty good player, so I looked out for him.

There was no doubt we had a pretty crowded outfield with Kingman, Milner, Rusty Staub, Del Unser, Gene Clines, and Jesus Alou. Rusty and Del were both hitting over .300, and Kingman was the big home-run hitter. With me coming back, it forced their hand in moving Kingman over to first and putting me back in left.

But I was in and out of the lineup after that, suffering with my injury. I really wasn't told how bad my knee was until later, when the trainer told me I should have had surgery long before I had it. All those in charge knew my knee had to be repaired and that I was only doing damage to it by continuing to play. I could play the outfield and could run, but hitting was the biggest problem because I had to alter my swing a little to compensate for the injury.

I wasn't ready to play on a daily basis, so I was relegated to pinch-hitting, and I believe I was perceived a certain way by Yogi. We had a meeting with Dr. Peter LaMotte (the team physician), Yogi, and me, where it was decided that, because of my knee problem, I needed to wear a brace before batting and in the field, and that I needed a warning ahead of time so I could put my knee brace on. I couldn't wear a brace comfortably while sitting on the bench for most of the game. I thought it had been made clear that I'd get a warning from Yogi if he was going to a use me. None of that happened. Then in Atlanta on July 18, 1975, everything changed.

Yogi called me to pinch-hit for Ed Kranepool in the seventh inning, and I kind of got upset about that, because Yogi gave me no warning. I lined out to short, then Yogi said I was in the game. Right away, I got pissed off because he didn't give me a warning about the knee brace and apparently hadn't thought about what was said in our meeting with the doctor, so I blew up.

I went into the clubhouse because I was upset at the way things were happening and the way they'd been happening all year. I was put on a certain regiment and would do certain things and get treatment, but none of the coaches or even the players were aware of it. Evidently, Yogi didn't share any of it with them. They knew nothing about my needing time to put on my brace or the meeting we'd had with the doctor. Now they were looking at me like I was faking it, that I didn't want to be on the field, that I was lazy, and this and that. So I had it out with Yogi—I mean, I blew up. We had a problem from that point on.

We finally met with management prior to a game, and Yogi brought his wife into the meeting along with the writer Dick Young and a few others. Well, I got pissed off about that. Yogi's wife had no business being at that meeting. She didn't know what the hell was going on, and what business did she have being in on a baseball meeting? I told them if Yogi's wife had o be in on the meeting, then my wife had to be there, too. She knows what I go through and what I've been through because she's been with me every day. Yogi's wife wasn't in the clubhouse or the dugout, why was she there? That's when I said I wouldn't play for Yogi anymore.

Yogi's wife was in the meeting and said Yogi loved me and we got along, and all that was true. I don't think Yogi did anything to me consciously that he thought would hurt me. I just thought it was a situation that could have been handled better by the front office. Having surgery on your knee is something that can change your career.

The day I left the hospital and came home, I was on my own. I thought I was young enough and strong enough that all I had to do was certain exercises, and things would be back to normal. Had it not been for all that had happened before I pinch-hit for Kranepool, I probably wouldn't have gotten pissed off like I did.

Yogi said it was the most embarrassing thing that had ever happened to him as a manager. I don't know what happened to him in the past as a manager, but I was the one who was embarrassed, because he wasn't protecting me. As I recall, we had a lot of people who had been pinch-hitting. A lot of times I'd be in the clubhouse getting treatment, and Joe Pignatano would come in and say I was supposed to be in the dugout, and I'd tell him I was where I was supposed to be, getting treatment. That's why I know he hadn't shared it with them, what we'd talked about with the general manager and the doctor. How was he embarrassed? I'm the one who got up and went out there, and when I came back to the dugout, he said I was in the game! No, I was the one who was embarrassed.

Yogi forgot about my situation. I wasn't wearing a brace. Had he given me warning so I could put it on, go pinch-hit, and then play in the outfield, that would have been fine. But he didn't do that as a manager. He called me at the last second and said, "Jonesey, you're pinch-hitting." That's when my blood started to boil.

I don't think anyone said Yogi was right, and I was wrong or vice-versa. Most of the players said it was a situation that should have been worked out, but I was being stubborn and so was Yogi. I don't feel any negativity toward Yogi or anybody else. All I know is the situation was poorly handled, because nobody was talking to each other. The doctor and the trainer had talked to me. Maybe they should have shared more with Yogi, or maybe he chose not to share it with the other coaches.

It just wasn't a good ending for my stay in New York. Don't get me wrong. Yogi was a decent person—he just didn't understand the gravity of the situation. And I revered his friendship, but I didn't think he did a good job with that. I said, "I'm not gonna play for Yogi again." They finally said they'd work out a deal with somebody, and I think they did, but I told them I wasn't interested. I was sick of baseball and the way I was being treated. I'll say it to this day, that M. Donald Grant hated to see that. He didn't really want to see me go. But Yogi was the manager.

We had moved away from the Florida incident, but I don't know if the fan base was still thinking about it when this happened and a bad pattern had started with me. I can understand why somebody would have an ill feeling about me, but there's always two sides to the story. Unfortunately, the first thing people read about what took place usually makes the most lasting impression.

I don't think what happened in Florida with the van incident had any bearing on what Yogi was thinking. Yogi wasn't that type of person. He was just in a situation, and maybe because I couldn't respond or do the kinds of things I'd been doing all those years, and he was in a pickle to win. I don't know his thinking. I do know I wasn't protected by him with the rest of the guys. I just can't go into his head and say he disliked me, because I don't think that's the case. I had a lot of respect for him, and I think he had a lot of respect for me.

If you knew Yogi, you can kind of figure the situation out. He wasn't Gil Hodges, and situations like that weren't his strong suit. I was sick of being lied to and thought I was being mistreated. Maybe I wasn't representing myself correctly. It could have been me. I just know that there was no reason for Yogi and me to be at odds. But there was turmoil.

First of all, you're the manager of a major league baseball team. Why the hell do you have to have your wife in a player meeting? That was the last straw. It had been going downhill, but that's when it came to a head. Yogi had always been a friend, and we'd always gotten along. He'd come to my locker and talk to me before all of this, even bring me ties and stuff like that, little gifts in appreciation. I'm a Yogi fan. Then after this meeting—and I said lots of stuff in the meeting I thought had to be said—I didn't think that his wife had a voice in any of this and kept wondering why she was there. I guess she was there in support of him, but I don't known why, as a manager you would even let his wife be in a situation like that. It wasn't that kind of a party where you bring your wife.

Dick Young wrote about that meeting in his column the next day, but I don't think any of the players knew who was in that meeting before it happened. Young called me "lazy," that I was "content to glide along on superior talent," and compared me to Joe Pepitone. That's hard for me to believe that Dick Young would write that. And how do you compare me to Joe Pepitone? Joe Pepitone was a good player, but I don't ever see where he was derelict in his duty. How do you say a player is not giving his all when the player isn't even on the field? At that time I wasn't even on the field that much because of my knee.

I've been everything but lazy. They said I was nonchalant and a lot of other things, but never lazy. That was just who I was and the way I looked to them. I've always known how to govern myself. I may have been the fastest man in baseball during that period, but I wasn't stealing bases. Why? Because we were on our own. There was nobody on the ballclub who could even teach the fundamentals of base-stealing. There were no batting coaches, no fielding coaches. There was nothing in baseball at that time, so people put a label on you. They said Hank Aaron looked like he was asleep at home plate. What did that mean? Because he was relaxed?

I remember being in Los Angeles once. I wasn't in the lineup that day, so I was taking extra batting practice with the bench crowd. There were a bunch of reporters and players behind the batting cage, and when I came up to hit, everybody was saying, "Look at how he hits. He's not falling all over himself, he's just so smooth."

But that wasn't the way I thought of myself. That's just me being me. That's the one fallacy that's followed the Black man throughout history. I've always known who I am. I've never been tired in a ballgame or at the end of a long season. I hear guys say, "I'm tired. I'm tired." I've never been tired because I don't tire myself out during pregame and all of those things. That doesn't mean that you're lazy. It just means you know who you are and what your capabilities are. And when you need to take extra time, you do that.

That's the White man's stereotype of Black people. It may be something that's passed down, but nobody has any business saying I was lazy. Nobody played as hard as I did. Nobody slid into home plate or second base as hard. But I didn't do Pete Rose, running down to first base or out to left field. That wasn't me—that was Pete Rose.

And that's why I told my wife I didn't want to read about me—I knew what I was doing. And I knew when I needed to do better, work harder so I could get better. I was the only one watching film as a hitter. They used to do it for pitchers, but I would go into the film room and watch not just my hitting, but my teammates so I could help some of them.

I stayed around for a couple of weeks after that, and then Yogi got fired a few weeks later. I don't know what management's thinking was, but Yogi gave an ultimatum that one of us had to go because I said I'd never play for him again. I said that because I'm a team player and respect management, but I lost all of that because of the way the whole thing went down.

I knew who I was dealing with. I knew who Yogi was. He was a good person but he wasn't a great manager, and maybe he would say I wasn't a great player. All of that may be true. I'm sure I would have played for him again in the right setting. In other words, if another meeting came up between me with all those same people in the room, I would've said, "Live and let live." I get mad sometimes and do and say different things. But I'm not a person who holds a grudge. I get over shit. I look at it and dissect it and move on.

I did move on from that, afterward when Yogi was in Houston. I went down there for an old-timers' game. I went over to him, and we talked like nothing had ever happened. I'm sure he got over it...I hope he did. But I got over it. And you would never hear me say anything bad about Yogi. He was a good person and good for baseball, but certain manager's instincts he didn't possess. I knew that, and everybody else on the ballclub knew that. The problem was communication. I guess he felt like I was dragging him through the mud and he was going to do some dragging back. When Yogi was fired soon after I was released, I thought that two people were gone from a good organization that could have survived together had there been meaningful dialogue.

We were having talks every day, and I pretty much asked for my release. I said I wouldn't play for Yogi again because of what had happened, and I didn't. The press in New York started to put words in my mouth. What you wouldn't say, they'd say it for you. I blame myself more than anybody else. I was just fed up, so I really asked for my release.

I had a bad taste in my mouth for the game because of what had happened. And what really hurt me was I wasn't given the proper information right off the bat. It wasn't the Mets' fault that I had a bad knee. It was somebody's fault that they didn't share how bad my knee was. I was having pain, and surgery wasn't talked about until the end of the year. It was never mentioned during the course of the year, and then I had someone tell me they knew my knee was bad and needed surgery after the year was over.

I didn't share that with anybody. I didn't go back and say the Mets screwed me up. I had a friend who wanted to sue them, but I said no to all that. He said they treated me unfairly, but I said they treated me as good as they saw the situation. It wasn't shared openly with management, they tried to hide it from me, and they hid it from themselves because they knew I needed to be on the field.

I don't blame anybody for my demise. It's on me. If I had to do this all over again, I would do it differently. I just should have leaned on people a little bit harder to get what I thought I needed to get back on the field. I just thought I could do everything by myself, and I couldn't.

Chapter 20

CHICAGO

AFTER THE METS released me in July 1975, I went home and started working out after resting my knee for a while. I was that kind of person. I ran every day, I worked out every day, things I'd always done and was used to doing all of my life, even as a teenager. I always knew how to take care of my body and to stay in shape, and I did it my own way.

Free agency was something new to us players, and I was free like a lot of guys were. I wasn't happy how my tenure with the Mets ended, how my Mets career that had been so wonderful before was now tainted from the van incident and then with Yogi. I wasn't sure if I even wanted to play baseball anymore.

The White Sox were the only team that reached out to me and invited me after the '75 season to try out for the team in spring training. I didn't have a structured contract and essentially had to make the team. I wasn't used to being in that kind of situation. I was focused on being myself again, loving the game again, and having the opportunity to start fresh in a new league with a new team, giving it my all.

When I went down with the White Sox and worked out in spring training, there was a strike that lasted a few weeks and put me in an even tougher position to make a good impression. But I tore it up in spring training. I think I batted over .600 and was hitting hard line drives just about every time I went to the plate. I think that surprised them—I don't think they were really ever serious about signing me. But my showing sort of forced their hand because they would have looked like fools if they hadn't signed me. They offered me a one-year deal just before the regular season started, and I was feeling part of the team for the first time.

I was ready to be the old Cleon Jones as a player and helping out with the core of good young players they had on the roster. The White Sox were going in a younger direction, but they didn't have a stabilizer on the team. Even though Ralph Garr had played a lot, he didn't study the game the way I did and wasn't the kind of guy who shared information on hitting like I did, maybe because he may not have had information on hitting the way I did. And Jorge Orta should have been a .300 hitter every year. He had it all, he just hadn't put to together.

With the permission of management, I was allowed to show them and others adjustments that needed to be made as to what they should do to be better. Even on the base paths, I was showing the players how to move off with the pitch, to keep the body in a package, how to stop, get back, or go forward.

I was explaining these techniques to the guys one day when our manager, Paul Richards, came over and thanked me. I was sort of a player-coach and enjoyed that dual role. I looked forward to helping develop the younger players. So I felt like I was being a good teammate and sharing my knowledge with the players—they seemed to appreciate it.

They had a nucleus with Garr, Orta, and Bucky Dent at short. And they had some great arms that kind of reminded me of the Mets staff of 1969, young arms like "Goose" Gossage, Terry Forster, and the veteran knuckleballer Wilbur Wood.

But Richards didn't utilize Gossage to his strengths, and his strength was in the bullpen, where he'd been quite successful just a year earlier. Sometimes when he started games, Goose couldn't get past the third inning. It was obvious to me that, with the kind of arm he had and his past success in the bullpen, he needed to be back where he was more comfortable. But they never could see what I and others saw, and they traded Gossage along with Forster in the off-season.

Goose said to me once that he could put the ball by me, and I said he couldn't. I told him he could trick me, but he couldn't throw the ball by me. We laughed and joked about it, then one day he was on the mound and asked me to get in the box to prove once and for all that he was going to throw it by me. I said go ahead and try. The harder he threw it, the harder I hit it.

He was a tremendous teammate and good baseball person because he was a winner. He wanted the ball all the time even then. He just didn't know what he possessed, because they thought he was a starter. He always pitched with all he had, but you can't do that over the course of nine innings. You've got to know how to adjust if you can throw 100 mph. You've got to know when to throw it and when not to, that you don't need to heat it up every pitch like he was doing. We all know the rest of that story.

Not only was I looking forward to playing and developing players, I was enjoying what I'd seen from the owner, Bill Veeck. You work for certain personalities in baseball, but for the short time I was with the White Sox, Bill Veeck was a breath of fresh air. He was somebody who was great for baseball because he was so innovative, like the old-look tops and the short pants the players wore later in the season for a few games. He was the type of owner who was delighted to take part in things. He put on a Revolutionary War uniform on Opening Day in 1976, during the nation's bicentennial celebration, and paraded around the field. It was fun seeing an owner participate and take part in the game of baseball. It truly showed to me that he was the kind of man that baseball needed. He was innovative in every sense of the word. He even brought Hank Greenberg and John Wayne around. I had a great deal of respect for his love for the game. All of that was refreshing, and I was looking forward to more of it throughout the season.

When we came north, I batted cleanup as the designated hitter on Opening Day at Comiskey Park. I went hitless but drew two walks, and we beat Kansas City 4–0. The next game in Minnesota (our doubleheader against the Royals was called on account of the cold), we faced their tough righty Bert Blyleven. Richards used the lefty Carlos May in the DH spot, and I sat the bench. Our third game I played left field, and Carlos DH'd again. I got my first hit as an American Leaguer off of Joe Decker, then got my first RBI the next day in Boston. Richards kept me in left field for the three-game series in Boston, but I went 1-for-11, and my average hovered around .100.

Of course, I wanted to get off to a good start. That's what every player wants. I'd had bad starts before, but the Mets always let me work through any early season slumps I was going through. And being that Carlos May was off to a bad start and hitting well below .200, there was no reason for me to believe my days as a White Sox were numbered. We were 4–2 at that point and heading to Yankee Stadium for a pair of day games. I wanted to be in the lineup, knowing I'd have a lot of New York fans and friends at the game to see me. But before the first game even started, I saw the handwriting on the wall.

Every year the Topps Baseball Card Company came around and got the rosters from management, indicating who was going to be there for the full year. A Topps representative would go around the locker room handing out gifts to those players named by management to pose for the baseball card photo. But they never came to me. I was passed over. When I wasn't offered a gift from Topps, I knew then—in New York—that something was up. As was the case with Yogi not telling the coaching staff about my knee problem and needing to wear a brace, nobody from the White Sox—including the manager—told me anything prior to that.

I thought about that for a while as I looked at the starting lineup and my name wasn't there. I pinch-hit in the eighth inning and drew a walk off of Tippy Martinez. I got cheers when I went to the plate, but it didn't feel right as just a pinch-hitter. I was used to playing every day and wanted to play every day. I knew it was early in the season, and I'd warm up before long. But what happened with Topps proved to be no accident.

I finally got my first two-hit game the next day off of Rudy May—two clean singles to center that brought my average up closer to .200. That's what happens early on in a season. A couple of bad games and you're batting .100. A couple of good games, and you can be up to .300. When we came back to Chicago for a homestand starting with the Red Sox, I was dropped to fifth in the order but got another hit. Then I went 3-for-4 against the Brewers the next day to raise my average to around .270. I felt pretty good about things, but then went 0-for-10 and dropped to .200. That's when our general manager, Roland Hemond, called me into the office.

As a player being called into the GM's office, things usually can go one of three ways: you're being sent to the minors, traded, or released. I knew going to the minors wasn't part of the deal, and being it was way too early in the season for any trades to be made, I knew I was about to be released.

Roland sat me down and told me he was the general manger, but they let the manager make roster decisions. He said he knew I was the best hitter on the ballclub and should be kept on the roster, but the club was going in another direction. I told him that was no problem and was kind of looking for it because of what happened with Topps. And just like that, my days with the White Sox were over.

I went out, packed my belongings, and started to think about what had just happened. If they were trying to win and develop a team, why wasn't I in the lineup every day? I went to spring training, knowing that I had to show I could do the job, and then hit over .600. Then I got released. That told me the only reason they signed me was that they had to because of what took place in spring training.

Richards didn't have anybody on that club who could swing the bat like I could, and everybody knew that. That was confirmed by the other coaches when they found out what happened. Minnie Minoso was the first to come over and said he'd never seen anything like it before, that he'd been in baseball a long time and it was rotten. He knew all the young guys were learning from me, and I was a good influence in the locker room. He said I was the best hitter on the team and everybody knew it—all the players knew it—and couldn't believe that the GM had no say in it. Then Jim Busby came over, just shaking his head in disbelief.

All the coaches loved and respected my ability, and they all talked about how wrong the whole thing was. When I came back out, all the guys came and shook my hand and said, "How can this happen? You're the best player on the team." I guess it was Paul Richards. Funny how it goes with managers. Yogi was fired right after I was released by the Mets, and Richards only lasted that one season.

I was fed up with baseball after that. In less than a year's time, I'd been released by two teams. That left such a sour taste in my mouth for the game. After I was released, I got calls from some teams to come talk and a lot of calls I wouldn't even take, I was fed up that much.

I was contacted by the Yankees to meet with the ballclub, and I told them I was sick of it. I didn't want to go through it anymore, so it never happened. Willie Mays was coaching for the Mets at the time, and I understand he had a conversation with George Steinbrenner, telling him that I was a good player and a good teammate and could help the Yankees. Gabe Paul got in touch with me right after that and told me to come to whatever town they were in at that time to work out a contract, but I never went. Playing in New York again would have been a good thing for me—the criticism from the writers and the fans never bothered me, and it wasn't the reason I never met Gabe Paul. I was simply sick of baseball and what had happened to me.

A lot of folks after that said I was blackballed by baseball, but I never thought it was anything like that. It was just baseball. I had signed with a young organization and went there with that mindset of forgiving and forgetting all that had happened just a few months earlier, and just concentrate on being a good player and being a good teammate.

I was teaching a lot to that young ballclub. I got a chance to engage with those players, and they could learn from me. I could stand behind the batting cage, and they'd come back to me and talk about hitting and whatnot—all of those things. It was a young ballclub, but I thought it was a good fit.

That was he hardest pill I've ever had to swallow, getting cut by the White Sox. I went to the White Sox with a job to do, I did it well, and then I was gone. I didn't pursue anything after that. I was just filled to the brim with not being heard, no being seen, not being taken care of by the organization. My playing days were over.

When I look back now at my short time with the White Sox, I thought I had six, seven, eight years left. I thought my better years were still in front of me. I look at Willie Mays, at Hank Aaron, at Tom Seaver—all of them went someplace else and started over. I just didn't know mine would be so short.

I've gotten past all of that long ago. The Mets organization has treated me well and is my organization for life. Even though I played in Chicago for that short time, and even though the end of my Mets career went the way it did, in my heart I will always be a Met.

Chapter 21

THE INSTRUCTOR

I WORKED FOR THE Mets for a few years in the early '80s as a roving batting instructor. It was fun, as well as the perfect job for me because my expertise was identifying flaws in the offense of a player—something I had always done, going as far back as the sandlots back home.

I was always able to retain whatever I'd been told when it came to hitting, and it felt natural for me to observe others and know right away what could help them become better. When I was with the Mets, I was the only one on the team watching film before and after games. I don't think it was something that was being done much around baseball at the time—at least not on my team. And I was watching film not only on myself but on my teammates so I could help them.

There were plenty of times when they'd swing and miss a pitch, and they'd look into the dugout for me, and I'd let them know what I thought they were doing. Everybody on our team knew I was a pretty good hitter and I was able to spot flaws and could help just about anyone improve. Everybody in the organization knew that, and that prepared me to become a hitting coach later on.

I knew before I even began teaching my hitting philosophy to these young hitters at Instructional Leagues that they'd been told their whole lives the pitcher was in charge of every encounter because they had the ball and knew what pitch they were about to throw. I started with changing that way of thinking, working first on reversing that concept before even heading out to the batting cages. I wanted those players to go up to the batter's box with a different mindset, that they were in charge no matter who was pitching that day, and to react to the ball, not the pitcher.

The baseball season is a long grind, and the mental part is the key to success for a player. Yogi Berra once said, "Baseball is 90 percent mental, and the other half is physical." It's funny, but we know what he meant, and he was right. I tried to convey to all those young hitters that the pitcher wants to be in control, but you are actually in control of your actions. The only way to be successful was by being prepared and being focused, and that by thinking you're in control, you are in control. If you look at all good hitters, whether it's Mickey Mantle, Hank Aaron, or Willie Mays, they always went to the plate with that confidence. Ted Williams thought, "If you throw it, I can hit it." Probably half the guys who go to the major leagues don't have that kind of confidence.

If there was a guy who was having problems hitting, I would seek that person out and get to the ballpark early and work with him. I'd first look at him taking batting practice or watch him in a game to determine something from each at-bat, looking for consistencies or inconsistencies. I'd study where he was being fooled or where his strengths might be. I'd look for tendencies on how he might react to a certain pitch. In three or four at-bats, you can learn a lot about a hitter.

The next day I'd take him out to talk and try and give him confidence and show him what it was I thought he was doing wrong or what he was doing right. Then I'd tutor him every step through that process. I'd stay for several games so I could see for myself and to be that person to give confidence to that player. I'd continue to instill that philosophy of being the one in charge and identifying flaws at the same time. If he wasn't doing exactly what we talked about or concentrating like I thought he should be, when he came back to the dugout, I would tell him. The next day we'd go out and work again on the same things. I found out that many young hitters made it harder on themselves because they were convinced that hitting was hard because they made it hard.

I had Lenny Dykstra in the Florida Instructional League in 1981 before he went on to play for Shelby in the South Atlantic League. Dykstra was a real project. He was a small guy who could run, a good outfielder with a decent arm who worked hard and loved the game. You couldn't work him too hard. But everything he hit was a fly ball, he wasn't driving the ball.

So we worked with him, got him to hit the top of the ball a little more, to be more patient at the plate in order to see the ball a little bit longer, and to use his God-given ability. He was a good student because he listened to what I had to say, and in no time at all he was pounding it. He became a good hitter because he realized the difference we were making with him, and he worked on it every day—that's when he took off and became a good player.

With him it took only a few days because he was so eager. I had Al Jackson pitch some batting practice to Lenny, and he hit a ball probably 400 feet, something I hadn't seen him do before. It was exciting to watch his reaction when he realized that it was there. He worked hard to stay in the majors and became a pretty good hitter. Before that time, he was in jeopardy of not getting to the big leagues—he had everything else, but he wasn't creating bat speed and didn't have any patience at the plate.

The Mets had a surplus of talented guys like Dykstra, Darryl Strawberry, Wally Backman, and Kevin Mitchell—guys who could hit. Strawberry was a few years ahead of Dykstra, but nobody needed to help him. He was a big talent and had a good swing. Everybody knew he was going to make it and make it big. Wally Backman was always a decent hitter, he just was his own worst enemy. He worked hard as a fielder and as a player, but he pretty much did his own thing. I knew how far I could go with a player and what he could take. Most of the time when a player needs you, they'll let you know that. Wally struggled at Tidewater, but we knew he was a decent player and was highly motivated.

Some of the players the Mets had throughout the organization were being released or about to be released, and one of them was Kevin Mitchell. The Mets wanted to release him. One or two of the coaches said he was a troublemaker and didn't think he'd ever reach the major leagues, so they recommended that he be released. I was called and asked what I thought about it, and I told the front-office to leave him alone, that I was going back to Florida in a week and would work with him. I could see that nobody thought they could handle him. They didn't want to take the time to get to know him and work with him on his attitude. I told them I could work with him and handle him, and so they agreed to let me try.

When I got back to Florida, I started right away by reading him the riot act, that he was being talked about by management in a less-than-positive way, and if he didn't wake up and do better he would be released. I took an interest in him as a person and as player because I saw the raw talent. I took him out a few times and found out he was afraid of the ball.

Once I found that out, I was able to talk with him and share with him information and knowledge of controlling the situation when seeing the ball. I told him everybody gets hit by a pitch once in a while, but if you put yourself in a position of control, you might still get hit from time to time but not in a way that it's going to hurt you.

So I told him I'd go to home plate and for him get on the mound and throw the ball at me deliberately. Oh, he didn't want to do that because he was afraid he would hit me. I told him he wasn't going to hit me, to throw at me as long as he could, and he wouldn't hit me because I was in control. After that, I asked him if he would allow me to get on the mound and throw at him, but he didn't want to do that because he was afraid I'd hit him. He got nervous about it.

What I was trying to teach him was he had to see the release point of the pitcher, and once he did, there was enough time to react and get out of the way. I showed him the release point and how to react to the ball, and that's what we worked on for a few days until he slowly overcame his fear of being hit. He gained confidence, went to Kingsport in the Appalachian League that year, and led the team in batting, home runs, and RBIs. He ended up on the Mets and in the World Series in 1986.

Here was a guy they wanted to release because somebody didn't recognize his talent, because they saw so many other things wrong with the person and the player. Later on, when he left the Mets, he became a star with the Giants, hitting 47 home runs and 125 RBIs in 1989, the year he was named the National League MVP. I saw him in New York that year when I came up for an old-timers' game. I had a conversation with Giants manager Roger Craig in the lobby of the hotel, and he thanked me for putting Kevin on the right path. And Kevin always acknowledged that. But that was my job. My job was to seek out the talent and develop it. He thanked me constantly, and he shared it with others.

Another special project I had was Mike Fitzgerald, a catcher who ended up going to Montreal in the Gary Carter trade. The Mets wanted to release him, said he'd never hit, and thought he wouldn't get out of A ball. He wasn't major league ready at the time, and the Mets knew it. So I told the Mets to give me some time with Mike, that hitting was the easiest part of the game, and I'd work with him on it. I stressed to them that you can't create a Bud Harrelson at shortstop or Tommie Agee in center field or a Mike Fitzgerald behind the plate, but you can make anybody a better hitter.

I worked with him when he was struggling at Tidewater before moving on to Jackson in the Texas League. I wasn't promising to make him a great hitter, but to make him a better hitter—good enough to play at the major league level—which was always my goal. I said all that to the farm boss, hoping they'd take a chance on him, but they kept saying they knew he played good defense but didn't think he'd improve enough as a hitter. But I wasn't backing down. I knew he was a project, but he had a few things in his favor that I knew were crucial to his development, and I told that to the Mets. Mike wanted to improve and become a better hitter, and was willing to listen and take my advice. With that mindset he was going to be easy to work with. I guess my stance was a convincing one. I worked with Mike on his hitting, and he started coming around. In fact, he ended up hitting over .300 that year for Jackson. Working with Mike was very gratifying, and it helped the Mets obtain Carter—a deal that probably wouldn't have happened without another catcher in the deal. It also led to Mike having a 10-year major league career.

We signed a bonus baby in 1982 named Terry Blocker, who went to Tennessee State, where he was coached by one of my home-boys, Alan Robinson. Terry had pretty good potential, he just couldn't hold the information we gave him. He had some success at Tennessee State, and everybody liked him. The problem sometimes is when you have some success, it's hard to make adjustments, and those old habits keep compounding. Most players have to make adjustments as they go into pro ball, but he wasn't able to retain enough of it.

When a guy is going good and then falls back on old habits by getting complacent and down on himself for getting into a little slump, it's important to keep building his confidence. But there are times when all the encouragement and confidence-building isn't enough. By that I mean it comes down to the player and his attitude and concentration and willingness to listen.

When I went down and worked with him at Jackson, he'd have good games as long as I was there. But as soon as I left, he couldn't keep it together. He just had a lot of bad habits. He was a good outfielder with a pretty good arm, great range in the outfield, but everybody wanted to be like Darryl Strawberry, hitting home runs. But he wasn't that kind of hitter. If I could have stayed with him every day, he would have become a solid major league player because he had it.

He ended up playing nine years in the minor leagues and parts of three seasons in the majors, and had some success in the minor leagues. But I maintain he could have been better than all of the guys picked ahead of him in the draft like Joe Carter and Kevin McReynolds and Matt Williams. He just needed reinforcement every day.

Most of the guys I worked with improved a lot when it came to hitting. That fact was proven time and time again when I worked in the Mets organization. Some of the coaches and managers called me the "Miracle Man." I'd go to a town where a player wasn't hitting, work with him, and when I left they were hitting and doing well.

An ironic coincidence was that Davey Johnson was the minor league manager in Jackson in 1981, when I was the hitting instructor, and we roomed together when I was in town. It had already been 12 years since I caught that last out of the 1969 World Series that he hit, and we talked about that last out all the time. He still maintained it was the hardest ball he'd ever hit in his life, and I just told him it was the weakest ball I ever caught. We joked and laughed about it, and knew it was amazing how we ended up together like we did for that short period of time.

There was no press about it at all. Nobody came around and asked how it felt after all these years later. It was just two guys put in a place at the same time with so much in common, linked by that play. As a matter of fact, when Davey left Florida on his way to Jackson, he had to come through Mobile, and he called me up and we met and talked like old buddies.

But after a few years as a roving instructor, it was all over for me with the Mets. They changed minor league affiliation, and with that a lot of jobs were lost. I certainly enjoyed my time teaching many hitters my philosophy of hitting, but I never heard from any other organization after that. It's all about making friends who later become managers or general managers, that sort of thing, and I guess I didn't make enough of them.

But when you know you've done a pretty good job, there's a great deal of satisfaction in that. Even when I was done as roving instructor many players used to call me and write me asking for help if they were struggling or in a slump. They'd tell me I meant so much to their progress and wanted to stay in touch. Not only does that give you the feeling that you know you had something to do with the success of that team, but that these guys always respected me and told me I made a difference in their lives. They became better ballplayers because of my teaching and my ability to give them intangibles that made a difference.

Sometimes management didn't try to access the people they employed and didn't totally understand how the relationships related to the development of a player. All they could see is the finished project and not the process. If anybody had looked at the kind of progress we made in that organization as it relates to developing hitters into big-league ballplayers, they might have made the decision to keep me on.

But I really didn't try to get in touch with anybody after that. I just decided that, if an opportunity presented itself, it would have to be back in the Mobile area. Coaching was always part of my lifelong dream. I've always wanted to be called "coach." I was inspired by my high school coaches and was in awe of the way they were able to handle an entire team of young men.

On Student Day of my senior year, my ideal situation was to emulate coaches Curtis Hardin, Charles Jackson, Charles Rhodes, and coaches Washington and Chapman. Some of them coached football, track, baseball, or basketball, and I played all of them. Because of that I had contact with all of them throughout the year. All of them were special to me—like fathers—because they had my interests in mind. I certainly admired them because they were good people and they took time and showed me the ropes. I even borrowed a tuxedo from Coach Jackson to go to the prom and took over his PE class on Student Day. They let students do that on that day. I was called "coach" that day, and I liked the way that sounded.

In 1983 I started volunteering for the baseball team at nearby Bishop State Community College. Coach Chapman was one of my baseball coaches in high school, and now he was coaching at the junior college level, so that was fun being back together again. I wasn't officially a coach until he asked me in 1986 to be his assistant. He brought me in to do what I love—teaching the fundamentals of the game and pitching batting practice. Along with coaching the Bishop State men's basketball team and being sports director for the school, I was busy enough at the time.

But I could see the need at the time for the women to have a softball team. Everything was for men at the college, except basketball. All of the junior colleges in the area instituted women's softball, and we were the last one to get a team. All of the Florida schools and most of Alabama and Mississippi schools had women's softball, but we didn't. So I started a team in 1994 and managed them that one season.

We had a great team that year. We were 46–16 and probably would have won the nationals the following year, but I left softball to go back to baseball full-time for a few years. The year I left, I left a championship-caliber team that ended up as runner-ups in just their second year.

But baseball was my strength, and I couldn't do both. The reason I didn't stay longer with baseball was recruitment issues. Bishop Sate was one of the few junior colleges that didn't have dormitories, so we couldn't bring people in from out of town and give them lodging and things of that nature, forcing me to recruit from just the local area. You could get decent players locally, but your super players—especially pitchers—coming from outside the area weren't interested in us because of our limitations. We couldn't compete without top pitching.

But there always seemed to be three or four players on your team who gave you joy and worked hard and moved forward to go to Grambling, Alabama State, or somewhere like that. I said earlier in the year that it would be my last. I didn't want to be there as a coach collecting a paycheck, because my emphasis was to win and produce talented players who became much better so they could move on when they left. But that wasn't happening, so it wasn't rewarding anymore.

But what I discovered were some great differences between coaching men and women. The women were more open to criticism—if you want to call it that—and more eager to work on making adjustments. They wanted to get better and felt the need to get better. Guys who played baseball in high school and batted

.310 or so thought they were good. If you don't hit .500 in high school, you may not be that good of a hitter. How many good pitchers do you face in high school? One or two? Not very many. Many of these guys were so set in their ways and so in tune with the information that they'd gotten from their high school coaches that they couldn't get away from it to get better.

I had a guy who thought he was a good infielder and could hardly catch a ground ball. And every time he missed one he had an excuse. Well, the excuse was he wasn't getting into position to play the ball and have good hand-eye coordination. I had one player who wasn't hitting well, and I got him to start adjusting and put him into position to hit well. He was hitting the ball out of the park, and all the other kids were saying, "Who is that?" And then he came to me the next day and said, "Coach, I don't feel good in that position." That tells me you're not dealing with a full deck if you don't see progress. If you don't feel good with progress, then you're in the wrong game. He didn't say he was going back to his own way, he just said he didn't feel comfortable. He had authority and was hitting the ball with authority. And that's what you had to deal with sometimes with some of these kids. But the good ones always listened.

I've been fortunate to have won some awards and to be recognized in a few halls of fame. In 1996 I won the Willie, Mickey, and the Duke Award; I was inducted into the Mobile Sports Hall of Fame in 1991, the Alabama Sports Hall of Fame in 2003, the Bishop State Community College Hall of Fame in 2019, and the New York State Baseball Hall of Fame in 2021. Being recognized is humbling and rewarding, a validation that you are being acknowledged for a job well done—and I'm proud of what I've done in baseball.

Chapter 22

COMMUNITY, *CLOTILDA*, AND OUR FUTURE

I KNEW WHEN I left my neighborhood that we were an underserved community and had been for some time. I've always known that Africatown had one direction to go and that was up. But as more time went by, things kept changing for the worse: the poverty level kept increasing, so many homes needed major repairs, and the younger folks were moving out. I thought the only direction it could go was up. But I was wrong. It went down.

Because we're surrounded by so much industry, it would have been prudent to pool resources and to team up to take advantage and to open up opportunity for our residents. But our leadership never worked as one to build and grow. Our so-called "leaders" had separate mindsets on how they could get people to invest in the community, close-minded and blind to the basic needs of the people—people working mostly in industries like the paper mill and the railroad. If you set out to conquer something and you're divided, you fail. There's been no pooling of mind-power to say, "Here we are as a community, and this is what we want." And because of that, we teeter on the brink instead of thriving or, at the very least, doing better.

When you don't have the financial wherewithal to make it happen, services and recreation facilities start closing down, people start moving out, vacant properties become an eyesore and a sign to outsiders that there's nothing here for them. Those who want to move out have lost significant property value. Most everybody who stays has no choice in the matter and are elderly folks living in a dying community with no finances to start over in another place. It bothers me and burns inside of me to see what has happened here, here in my community that I love so much.

As if our residents didn't have enough to worry about, Mother Nature hadn't been kind, either. Over the course of only two-and-a-half years, Tropical Storm Alberto and Hurricanes Sally and Zeta came through here. Roofs were gone and needed replacing. Houses were battered and needed painting, repairs to piping, removal of water-logged carpets, and more. Debris needed to be cleared. Trees needed to be planted. The elderly needed help getting to appointments, to the grocery store, to a job, whatever it may be. Historic structures needed to be preserved. Homeowners with no insurance, no savings, and often no dependable, decent-paying jobs were hit hardest. So that's when I decided to do something about it. I just had to do something more to help.

Some were more interested in themselves and how they could benefit. But about 15 years ago, we felt the call and knew that we needed to come together, and God knows there was outside influence stopping us from moving forward. That's when my wife and I and other people in the community said, let's do what we can do no matter how small it may seem. If we work in a community where people can see the work we're doing, they'll be more apt to join in and help move the community forward—fixing roofs and windows and floors and doors, painting houses, and clearing the land. After I secured a a 501(c)(3) nonprofit organization for the community, everybody knew in a hurry who they had to get in touch with. When you come up in a close-knit community with a radius of 15 miles, everybody knows everybody else.

So industry started to call and asked how they could help. It took a while for us to get there, and it might seem small to the average person, but that was a big hurdle for this community. Right now we have six or seven different organizations saying they represent this community, yet some of them don't know Edwards Street from Front Street and probably haven't been into the community 20 times in total. You're fighting all of that. People do things for reasons and often times it's for money or fame. I have a famous name, so I'm not living for that. We're not looking for something for the Jones family, we're looking for something for the neighborhood.

People who'd lived here and moved out had always expressed a desire to come back, but the building codes were strict and many of the houses sat on vacant land. For years we didn't have any building going on, and so many of the abandoned buildings needed to be demolished. We're trying to save some of it, because if you destroy it all you risk losing your historic significance. We're mindful of that, so whatever we can save, we save.

Africatown is part of Mobile, in the second of the city's seven districts. There are 19 neighborhoods in District 2. Each of us have a representative on the city council. My goal is to work strictly in this neighborhood to try and make a difference by drawing people back in, so I have no interest in being a city council member. I wanted to be available at all times being in charge of the crews as well as being a worker. So I formed the Last Out Community Foundation to subsidize the neighborhood.

My wife and son and daughter have been pushing me for years to do it. We've had golf tournaments and things like that before and we were able to use those funds to put roofs on people's houses. We were able to refurbish houses and put together projects to bring people back into the community who had to leave because their property was in disarray. The first year of the foundation was 2019, but long before that we worked with the mayor and city council to do the little things that could be done through the state like the Fortified Roofing Project.

We're a conduit for all these things now. I've said this many times that people know who to contact for help when they respond. Before that, they knew I lived in the neighborhood but didn't know I was this involved in helping the community. If they've got questions now, they can knock on my door or call me up. There's not even a grocery store around, and the closest Walmart is six or seven miles away, so we put in a neighborhood pantry and give out food a few days a week—that's a hurdle we've tried to cross for a while. It's close enough now that people can walk or ride a bicycle to get there.

It's a hard day when we go out to fix a roof or to clear a property, but it's so worthwhile. We start off at 8:00 in the morning with our volunteers, and in the summertime we start at 7:00. My job is to make sure they know where they're going and what has to happen on that particular day. It's important that everyone try to respect the situation because we're working for people and they're depending on me. We still have plenty of 90-year-olds living here who I know personally, people I grew up idolizing as a kid. I feel a real obligation to help repopulate, regenerate, and grow the community by putting forth the effort to build and refurbish homes and really try to take the time to save historic structures.

I'm blessed to be able to give my time to this cause, but you've got to have a team willing to go the last mile with you. I do have some people my age and younger who are working with us, but most of the time the young folks have families to support and have to work. They need to make sure they take care of their own families, and by all means come seek us out if and when they can. I scrounge up money when I can give them something.

When you're talking about people spending six, seven hours, or more per day, everybody's time is worth something, even volunteers. Often times they say no, I just want to volunteer. That's the heart of Africatown speaking.

There's so much more that needs to be done here that we've become involved in. We have youth baseball in and around the area, and we have a park, so we do have youth sports, but interest in playing baseball is nothing like it was when I came up. There were kids everywhere back then, mostly boys. The street that I was on had 50–75 kids because people had nine or 10 kids per family. One family had 22, and another had 19. You could go outside your house and throw a ball up to yourself, and by the time it landed in your hands, you'd have two teams.

But all that has changed dramatically. We have about seven or eight schools in the inner-city with no baseball program. Football is king in Alabama, but we've got a lot of talented kids. The problem is, once they get out of Pee Wee Football at age 12, there's nothing for them, and that's when they need attention the most. We're trying to formalize a program where we can target those kids in all sports—boys and girls—in baseball, football, softball, and volleyball. Our goal is to make it a city-wide program to make sure we give those kids the attention they need and keep our hands on them through high school. We held our first Cleon Jones Legends Baseball Camp clinic last year and had more than 60 kids and 10 coaches—including another local player, Jake Peavey—working with me. It was a fantastic success and the start of something bigger. You have to find time for the people who need you, like the way people found time for me when I needed them.

That's why I fight so hard today for my community and why all of my thoughts each and every day are to try to further enhance and develop the community that made me. I'll never forget the people who helped further my development by providing a space and an avenue to help develop my skill and mindset enough to become a major league player. As a player and a person, I knew all along I owed that all that to my community and would one day give back.

For a few years now, we've sponsored the Cleon Jones Celebrity Golf Tournament to raise money and had great support from Rod Gaspar, Ron Swoboda, Ed Kranepool, Wayne Garrett, and Bobby Pfeil. The Mets were a major sponsor a few years ago and gave all kinds of giveaways plus a nice monetary gift. I haven't yet reached out to Major League Baseball, but that day is coming.

About six years ago I started thinking about all the Hall of Fame players from our area and how unusual it seemed to so many people around the country who noticed that and wanted to talk about it. I was always proud to be associated with Satchel Paige, Hank Aaron, Willie McCovey, Billy Williams, and later Ozzie Smith, so I approached our mayor with an idea.

I reminded him that New York had 8 or 9 million people, but we had more Baseball Hall of Famers with a population of 200,000, and that we should do something to honor that and to draw tourists to the area. He seemed interested enough and asked me to sketch it out for him and then bring it back when I was finished. I started to put together collages, then thought about adding other players from Mobile to fill it out more, like a complete team. By the time I finished, there were at least 23 names on the collage, and when I presented it to him, it blew him away.

From there, more people became involved, and the idea grew substantially. What started out as a possible memorial for our five Hall of Fame baseball players turned into facilitating a tourist attraction in how it relates to Mobile sports—our baseball, football, and basketball legends, and even now our Olympic champions. The baseball concept included myself, Tommie Agee, Tommie Aaron, Amos Otis, Jake Peavey, and Juan Pierre. After many discussions with others, I suggested putting in a Walk of Fame somewhere near the riverfront where people could walk along the riverfront or boardwalk, dine at a special restaurant and be near other entertainment—family-friendly so people could enjoy our history. That all came together in January 2021 when Mobile mayor Sandy Stimpson and councilman John Williams announced plans at Cooper Riverside Park for the construction of the statues and full-sized busts. We have a long way to go with it, but are thrilled an idea has become a reality.

While all this was going on, the search continued on for the *Clotilda*. People always seem surprised when they find out about my interest in the *Clotilda* and in what I've been doing with my life. People remember me as a baseball player and always will. I never talked about the *Clotilda* or my community much when I played baseball, but that doesn't mean I wasn't thinking about it, because I was. I hoped and prayed that one day the *Clotilda* would be found, that the hand of God would help us out. It wasn't just for the historic significance or showing proof that it existed to all the naysayers—but a part of me knew that such a find could help stimulate the local economy and help it grow.

I'd long envisioned the wreck being found, pulled from the water and restored, but that would be costly, and it been under water for so long. Few people were still looking for it, but a local reporter—Ben Raines—was one of them. I knew Ben had thought he'd found it in a different part of the river from where he thought it might be, but it wasn't the *Clotilda*. We found out later from Ben that he had been looking for it for a while and had a premonition one morning to get up and go look for it again at low tide. That was when he found something significant.

He was setting out for 12-Mile Island, where my grandparents and uncles and cousins had a camp house and used to go up on the weekends to fish and hunt and make white-lightning. I had fished that area quite a bit as a youngster and as an adult, but never considered that the *Clotilda* could be in that area. I was surprised when he did find something. God almighty put it in Ben Raines's mind to go to that area to find the ship.

The wreck he found was covered mostly in mud, where it had been resting for years. He looked at it, measured it and did all the things that could help identify it. When he presented his findings to the experts, they said the ship was to long, too this, too that. Almost a year later on May 22, 2019, after researchers analyzed artifacts pulled from that ship, it was confirmed—the *Clotilda* had been found.

When I first found out it was true, I did a little dance and went out there to see for myself with two others connected to the find on a small motor boat. By then the TV networks had got wind of it and were there and asked some questions. It soon turned into a restricted area. They set up cameras around the area so nobody could enter except people who were designated to go there.

Then the Smithsonian and our congressman and senator, Doug Jones, got deeply involved in it. Finances were set aside by the government to try and raise it or enshrine it. After more time, it was determined there'd be no way to raise it up. The ship was so fragile if would pull apart from itself with ease. Its deck had been set on fire, but the hull was intact. When I found that out, I thought they could still enshrine it where it lies, build a monument and conduct tours to the site. But when ideas like mine and others came around, other ideas—from a mostly white group—suggested building a replica and sending it up and down the river with tourists. My first thought was, *Who wants to see a slave ship going upon and down the Mobile River?*

The white population looks at it as a slave ship, but these were people who were enslaved, pulled away from their country for the purpose of slavery. I've always called it a human cargo ship for the purpose of enslaving folks. These people never committed a slave act. We know that it happened, but we have to get over the fact that we don't want to talk about slavery and human trafficking. If we face the fact that these things happened then we can get past bringing up slavery and saying what many in the white population don't want to deal with. If you say that your great-great-grandparent was a slave owner and a hater, that has nothing to do with who you are. That reflects the times.

Everybody from presidents on down had slaves. Why are you fearful of facing the fact that slavery existed and was a part of what our country was at that time? History ought to be complete and be the correct history we learn, not that history that favors a particular race. Let's print history as it happened. Let's direct it, move on, try to get better from it and establish some sort of memorial or visitors' center and show people of all colors what happened here.

We came to an understanding, and that's what we're working on now. At some point in time we're planning on building a replica of it and have a reenactment of it as part of the tourism. If this all works out, that means funds are coming in to revitalize the entire community. Whatever artifacts are there, chains and whatever else they can find, we need to see and touch. We need to understand better what these people went through on their voyage.

Look what's happened here in just a short time. My foundation became a reality, they found the *Clotilda*, and we're building statues of our best athletes. It's exciting and rewarding and equally important to Angela and me to keep all this going, to be part of all of it. There's so many needs here with so many possibilities to build and grow and to remind. I've gotta stay healthy, and with the blessings of the Almighty, we can get some things done.

Chapter 23

FINAL THOUGHTS

WHEN I WAS COMING home after the 1969 World Series, I hardly had a New York minute to reflect on what we'd just accomplished. There were so many distractions with people yelling and screaming happily, people crying and sharing with us—in their own way—the spoils of victory. People were speaking in cliches like, "We slayed the dragon," or, "We took down Goliath"—whatever came to mind.

When I arrived back home, the city of Mobile welcomed us back with a huge parade. Tommie, myself, Amos, and even Billy Williams from the Cubs were there, along with thousands of people lining the streets. Later, we all spoke to the crowd, sharing some of our thoughts about the season. We talked about it briefly when we had the chance to be together, and to a man none of us had ever felt like this in our lifetime—and never would again. We were young and on top of the world...exhilarated yet numb ...energized yet humbled...thankful yet speechless. If there ever was such a thing as Cloud Nine, well, we were on it.

I found myself at such times reflecting on those who came before me, and this was no exception. My community and its people and those who came before always were with me in everything I did. And now seeing so many family, friends, and neighbors lining the streets of Mobile, well, it went to another level.

Of course, I thought about Jackie Robinson, because without Jackie, there'd be no parade in Mobile. I though about my parents who left home when I was just a child, never to return; Grandma Myrt and all those others who made Cleon Jones; sweeping images coming to mind with every wave from the crowd. As I studied the faces and the smiles and saw the tears rolling down so many cheeks, I was pleased at what I saw—both Whites and Blacks coming together to celebrate together—an image unlikely to have happened here in my lifetime. But now it had.

I've been awed at how the human mind works at times, how it is able to generate a myriad of thoughts all at once, and mine was working overtime. I understood that this celebration had deeper meaning beyond the New York Mets, beyond Cleon Jones. It was a celebration of people, a celebration of mankind, and the capacity within ourselves to help make a change. And as the shouting and the waving and the honking of horns continued, my mind went to Martin Luther King.

We were in San Francisco when we heard about his death. The games were postponed, and it had an affect on all of us. There was so much unrest during those times, and the makeup of the country was more polarized than as it is now, but we started feeling good about race relations because of Dr. King. I could feel it and see it even in the streets, kids playing baseball, Blacks and Whites saying, "I want to be Tommie Agee," or, "I want to be Cleon Jones." We never saw that before. None of us knew what the fallout would be. We didn't know what was going to take place with race relations and what would happen to the country.

Dr. King had been killed by a White man. But my White teammates rallied around us—authentically feeling what we were feeling—anger, bitterness, and wondering what was next. When we got together and talked about it, there was so much sympathy, and I knew they could feel what I was feeling. If a team of baseball players could feel that way—brothers always—I felt good that progress would continue.

No more than a few seconds passed by as those thoughts occurred to me. I looked to the streets just then and thought about Dr. King's march from Selma to Montgomery in 1965—places not far from here—and wondered what he'd be thinking if he could see this now.

As I reflect on everything that happened to me as a player and as a man, the person most responsible for keeping me in line and staying by my side is Angela—my beautiful wife of 56 years. Every team and every marriage needs a stabilizer, and Angela is the stabilizer in our family. When I was having my troubles with Yogi and the incident in Florida with the parked van, Angela rolled with each and every punch that was thrown our way, and knew how to repel all of that and stay strong. No matter what happened and what people were thinking, Angela was always there to hold my hand and remind me that we'd get through this and that we had to think about family.

She was not just a stabilizer, she was a motivator. When horrible things were written in the paper about me, she'd read them and always took the high road. She never told the kids, "Your daddy's doing something wrong." Instead, she found a way to always put the family in a good light. She's the reason why we've been married for over 56 years. There were times that I was just being selfish about things, but I've always been mindful of my family because I've always loved her and my kids. Sometimes you get lost in your celebrity status, I guess.

You get lost sometimes, and somebody has to reach up and tap on your shoulder and say there's more to life than this, there are others in your life affected by what you do. She certainly was there for all of it. She said that we were made to be together, that she chose me because I was the person that she thought God made for her. Certainly when I look at that and think about it, I don't know of a better mate anybody could have. She said the Lord Almighty put us together, and I believe that.

At our old-timers' games, Ernie Banks used to always ask everybody, "You still got a wife?" Then, "Do you still have the same wife?" I'd answer him that I was still married with the same wife, and he'd say, "Man, you're lucky. I don't have the same wife, and none of my friends got the same wife. You're lucky." He said it in a kidding way, but he brought that to my attention, and I knew he was right. I was lucky.

I'm fortunate. I know that my family is No. 1 to me. I've always known that. But after fifty-some years you see your kids grow and then your grandkids and your great-grandkids grow, you think about all of that. It's like the duck on the water—it's smooth on the top, but there's a whole lot of kicking going on underneath. There was a lot of kicking going on, but Angela always kept it smooth on the top.

We have a great relationship with our kids, Anja and Cleon Jr., and we're a family that's intact. We're a family that believes in life and in the pursuit of happiness, and we believe in each other. We believe in our fellow man, all the way down the line with five grandkids and one great-grandchild. My grandkids are into football. I'm not bothered at all that there are no baseball players. I bring it down to what they want and what I want to see. What I want to see is getting a thorough education, to be a good student and good steward, that's what I preach. If you want to play a sport, play it. But if you don't want to play a sport, don't play it because of me.

I don't know where to start when it comes to those who've passed. I found out recently more than 100 are gone from my managers, front-office people, broadcasters, and teammates, with hundreds more from other teams. I may not know exactly when